ضرب المثل های دری افغانستان

Zarbul Masalha:
151 Afghan Dari Proverbs

دنیا با امید زنده است.

Doonya baa omeed zenda ast.

The world is alive with hope.

ضرب المثل های دری افغانستان

Zarbul Masalha:
151 Afghan Dari Proverbs

THIRD EDITION
Includes 50 Bonus Proverbs

Collected and translated by
Captain Edward Zellem
United States Navy

Edited by
Aziz Royesh

Illustrated by
The students of Marefat High School
Kabul, Afghanistan

Cultures Direct Press

Third Edition
Published in the United States of America
by Cultures Direct Press
A Division of Cultures Direct LLC

Second Edition Published 2012
in the United States of America
by Cultures Direct LLC

First Edition Published 2011
in the Islamic Republic of Afghanistan
by Karwan Press

Library of Congress Control Number: 2015904838
Cultures Direct Press, Tampa, FL

ISBN-13: 978-0986238604
ISBN-10: 0986238600

Dedication

This book is respectfully dedicated
to the people of Afghanistan,
and to those who are working together with them
to bring lasting peace and security.
May Almighty God bless and protect them
in this difficult task, and bring them success.

اهداء

این کتاب، با کمال احترام، به مردم افغانستان و آنهایی که همراه با آنان
برای تأمین صلح و امنیت پایدار تلاش می‌کنند، اهدا می‌گردد.
خداوند آنها را در این مأموریت دشوار، مشمول رحمت، عنایت و توفیقات
خویش قرار دهد.

As the Proverb says:

چنانچه این ضرب‌المثل می‌گوید:

کوه هر قدر بلند باشد، سر خود راه دارد.

Koh har qadar beland baashad, sar-e khod raah daarad.

Even if a mountain is very high, it has a path to the top.

موفق باشید
Mowafaq Bashid
Be Successful

More books by Edward Zellem

Mataluna: 151 Afghan Pashto Proverbs

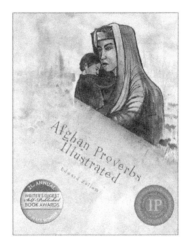

Afghan Proverbs Illustrated

Winner of 8 international book awards
Now available in 15 languages and over 100 countries

Praise for Afghan Proverbs

"Ed's Afghan Proverb books are a personal project, and some people say that they help win hearts and minds. I have always thought that 'winning hearts and minds' is an inaccurate way to say it, because *winning* implies that somebody also *loses*. Nobody loses here. I think Ed's Afghan Proverbs books *connect* hearts and minds, which is a truly critical task."

General David H. Petraeus (U.S. Army, Ret.)
Former commander of U.S. and ISAF forces in Afghanistan

"These proverbs are a reminder of old traditions and folklore that have been passed from generation to generation. And they are a true delight for anyone who has been away or alienated from Afghanistan."

Leena Alam
Award-winning Afghan actress and UNAMA Peace Ambassador

"An informative and beautifully produced volume of Afghan proverbs that Edward Zellem collected in Afghanistan during his time of service there as a captain in the United States Navy. His collection represents a treasure of the proverbial wisdom of that country, and serves as an example of the commonality of life that ties humanity together all over the world."

Dr. Wolfgang Mieder
Professor of German and Folklore, University of Vermont
Internationally recognized proverbs scholar and author

"Captain Zellem's collection is an outstanding work that underscores our common humanity."

Dwight Jon Zimmerman
New York Times #1 best-selling author

"All types of social and cultural learning and understanding are enriched through Proverbs."

Nancy Dupree
Philanthropist, historian, author, and founder of the Afghanistan Centre at Kabul University (ACKU)

فهرست مطالب

Table of Contents

Foreword	i-iv	پیشگفتار
Preface	v-xxiii	مقدمه
Introduction	xxiv-xxv	پیشگفتار
Dari Facts	xxvi-xxvii	نکته هایی درباره ی زبان دری
Pronunciation Guide	xxviii-xxix	رهنمای تلفظ
The Dari Alphabet	xxx	لفبا دری
The Proverbs	1-151	ضرب المثل ها
About Sufi Ashqari	152-153	در باره ی صوفی غشقری
50 Bonus Proverbs	154-204	۵۰ ضرب المثل های اضافی
Appendix	205-209	ضمایم
About the Author	210	درباره ی مولف
About MHS	211-212	در باره ی معرفت
About the Editor	213	در باره ی ویراستار
About the AIP-IAP	214	در باره ی AIP-IAP
Photos	215-218	عکس ها
The Artists	219	هنرمندان
Index	222-223	فهرست

پیشگفتار

Foreword by
General David H. Petraeus (U.S. Army, Ret.)

Proverbs and sayings are the linguistic equivalent of a "key terrain district," a place where culture and language meet. This is certainly true in Afghanistan, where Afghan proverbs and their use so profoundly reflect the people and their character.

This book reveals the richness of meaning and human emotion found in Afghan proverbs. These proverbs provide insights into the resilience, independence, and pride that have enabled Afghans to survive and overcome innumerable challenges over the years. Indeed, Afghans have suffered much over the last thirty years, in particular, as well as during many periods prior to the past three decades. However, they have also achieved a great deal over the centuries, during which they have displayed the remarkable combination of strength, faith, and optimism that has carried them through the hard times. These traits are in full view in the richness and variety of Afghan proverbs.

As a student of world cultures for several decades, I have long recognized the need for cultural understanding between peoples. This is especially true when those peoples are working together to achieve common goals. In view of this, and to foster mutual understanding here in the shadow of the Hindu Kush, the United States created the "Afghan Hands" program in 2009. This program helps improve Afghan-American relationships by immersing an elite group of US military officers in Afghan languages and culture before they deploy, and by then assigning them to positions here in Afghanistan where their expertise can be used to best effect. Upon completion of their tours here, they are assigned to billets in the United States that make use of, and help to maintain, their Afghan expertise.

Captain Edward Zellem of the United States Navy was among the first of our Afghan Hands to deploy to Afghanistan. His personal interest in and clear love of Afghans and Afghanistan, together with his impressive understanding of Afghan ways, are representative of the best of our Afghan Hands.

This book began as a personal hobby for Ed, and it then blossomed into a wonderful example of how cultures can be bridged - at the human level, person to person. Indeed, I have found, as Captain Zellem has, that the *process* of understanding and the *willingness* to understand are fundamental to effective communication, the establishment of true friendships, and the development of sincere partnerships. In fact, a foreigner who reaches out to an Afghan with trust, respect, and genuine interest will almost always be greeted with the same in return. Knowledge and use of Afghan proverbs can be an effective tool in such outreach.

I am very pleased to be able to introduce Captain Zellem's book to the Afghan people and to coalition forces. In so doing, I emphasize recognition that, as we work together to help our Afghan colleagues bring peace and security to this great nation, we must always try to understand each other as friends, partners, and, most importantly, fellow human beings. As one of the Proverbs in the book states, "Dil ba dil roh darad" - دل به دل راه دارد - "There is a way from heart to heart."

I hope you enjoy the book as much as I have.

General David H. Petraeus
Commander, NATO International
Security Assistance Force
and U.S. Forces-Afghanistan

April 2011

قوماندانی
نیروهای بین المللی کمک به امنیت (ایساف)
نیروهای ایالات متحده – افغانستان
کابل، افغانستان

پیشگفتار توسط سترجنرال دیوید اچ پترییس

ضرب المثل ها و گفته ها مشابه لسانی " مناطق مهم کلیدی " میباشد، یعنی جائیکه فرهنگ و لسان باهم تلاقی می نمایند. در افغانستان، جائیکه ضرب المثل های افغانی و نحوه استفاده آنها انعکاس دهنده مردم و شخصیت شان میباشد، این امر بطور قطع یک حقیقت است.

کتاب هذا غذاء معنوی و احساس بشری موجود در ضرب المثل های افغانی را نشان می دهد. این ضرب المثل ها ارائه دهنده نگرش درونی بر قابلیت ارتجاعی، استقلالیت و احساس غروری میباشد که افغان ها را بر آن داشته است تا در جریان سال ها بقاء یافته و بر مشکلات بی شمار غالب آیند. یقیناً، افغان ها در جریان سی سال گذشته بطور اخص و همچنان بسیار دوره های قبل از این سه دهه متحمل نشواری های بسیار شده اند. اما در جریان قرن ها که آنها دست آوردهای زیادی نیز داشته اند، قرن هائی که آنان ترکیب، قابل ملاحظه قدرت، ایمان و خوش بینی را از خود به نمایش گذاشته که آنها را در دوران مشکلات به پیش رانده است. این خصایص در غذاء و تنوع ضرب المثل های افغانی بطور کامل مشاهده می گردد.

منحیث یک محصل فرهنگ های جهان در چندین دهه، من به نیاز به درک فرهنگی میان مردمان را به خوبی دریافته ام. این امر مخصوصاً زمانی واقعیت دارد که این مردمان در کنار یکدیگر فعالیت می کنند تا به اهداف مشترک نائل آیند. با توجه به این امر و به منظور ارتقای تفاهم دو جانبه در سایه سلسله جبال هندوکش، ایالات متحده امریکا در سال 2009 پروگرام دستان افغان (Afghan Hands) را ایجاد کرد. این پروگرام از طریق آموزش لسان های افغانی به تعدادی از افسران نظامی نخبه امریکائی قبل از اعزام شان و سپس توظیف آنان به وظایفی در افغانستان، جائیکه مهارت آنها می تواند به بهترین نحو مورد استفاده قرار گیرد، کمک می نماید تا ارتباطات افغان ها و امریکائی ها بهبود یابد. بعد از اینکه مامورین خویش را در اینجا به پایان رسانند، آنها به وظایفی در امریکا توظیف می شوند که بتوانند از مهارت خویش در مورد افغانستان استفاده کرده و به آنها کمک گردد تا این مهارت های خویش را حفظ نمایند.

دگروال ادوارد ذالم مربوط نیروهای بحری ایالات متحده از جمله اولین گروپ پروگرام دستان افغان (Afghan Hands) بود که به افغانستان اعزام گردید. علاقه شخصی و عشق آشکار وی به افغان ها و افغانستان در کنار درک گذار ایشان از روش های افغانی نمایانگر دستان افغان میباشد. در اوایل این کتاب منحیث یک کار سرگرمی شخصی برای او ادوارد بود و سپس در قالب الگوی فوق العاده ای شکوفا نمود مبنی بر اینکه چگونه می تواند در سطح بشر، میان اشخاص، پل در بین فرهنگ ها ایجاد شود. . من نیز یقیناً همانند دگروال ذالم دریافته ام که پروسه درک نمودن و تمایل به درک کردن نهداب ارتباطات موثر، ایجاد دوستی واقعی و انکشاف همکاری های صادقانه میباشد. در واقع یک شخص افغانی که با یک افغان با حس اعتماد، احترام و علاقه مخلصانه روی می آورد، تقریباً همیشه در مقابل همانگونه با وی برخورد می شود. دانستن و استفاده ضرب المثل های افغانی می تواند در این رویکرد یک ابزار موثر باشد.

من بسیار خرسندم از اینکه می توانم کتب دگروال ذالم را به مردم افغان و نیروهای ائتلاف معرفی نمایم. در این راستا، من روی شناخت این امر تاکید می نمایم که، همانگونه که ما در کنار یکدیگر فعالیت می نماییم تا همکاران افغان خویش را در آوردن صلح و امنیت برای این ملت بزرگ کمک کنیم، ما باید همیشه سعی نماییم که یکدیگر را منحیث دوستان، شرکاء و از همه مهمتر بشر همنوع درک نماییم، چنانچه یکی از ضرب المثل های موجود در کتاب می گوید: " دل به دل راه دارد".

امیدوارم که شما نیز به اندازه من از کتاب لذت ببرید.

سترجنرال دیوید اچ پترییس
قوماندان نیروهای بین المللی کمک امنیت (ایساف) ناتو
و نیروهای ایالات متحده – افغانستان

The original foreword by General Petraeus in Dari

HEADQUARTERS
International Security Assistance Force/
United States Forces-Afghanistan
Kabul, Afghanistan
APO AE 09356

Foreword by General David H. Petraeus

پیشگفتار توسط سترجنرال دیوید اچ پتریس

Proverbs and sayings are the linguistic equivalent of a "key terrain district," a place where culture and language meet. This is certainly true in Afghanistan, where Afghan proverbs and their use so profoundly reflect the people and their character.

This book reveals the richness of meaning and human emotion found in Afghan proverbs. These proverbs provide insights into the resilience, independence, and pride that have enabled Afghans to survive and overcome innumerable challenges over the years. Indeed, Afghans have suffered much over the last thirty years, in particular, as well as during many periods prior to the past three decades. However, they have also achieved a great deal over the centuries, during which they have displayed the remarkable combination of strength, faith, and optimism that has carried them through the hard times. These traits are in full view in the richness and variety of Afghan proverbs.

As a student of world cultures for several decades, I have long recognized the need for cultural understanding between peoples. This is especially true when those peoples are working together to achieve common goals. In view of this, and to foster mutual understanding here in the shadow of the Hindu Kush, the United States created the "Afghan Hands" program in 2009. This program helps improve Afghan-American relationships by immersing an elite group of US military officers in Afghan languages and culture before they deploy, and by then assigning them to positions here in Afghanistan where their expertise can be used to best effect. Upon completion of their tours here, they are assigned to billets in the United States that make use of, and help to maintain, their Afghan expertise.

Captain Edward Zellem of the United States Navy was among the first of our Afghan Hands to deploy to Afghanistan. His personal interest in and clear love of Afghans and Afghanistan, together with his impressive understanding of Afghan ways, are representative of the best of our Afghan Hands. This book began as a personal hobby for Ed, and it then blossomed into a wonderful example of how cultures can be bridged – at the human level, person to person. Indeed, I have found, as Captain Zellem has, that the process of understanding and the *willingness* to understand are fundamental to effective communication, the establishment of true friendships, and the development of sincere partnerships. In fact, a foreigner who reaches out to an Afghan with trust, respect, and genuine interest will almost always be greeted with the same in return. Knowledge and use of Afghan proverbs can be an effective tool in such outreach.

I am very pleased to be able to introduce Captain Zellem's book to the Afghan people and to coalition forces. In so doing, I emphasize recognition that, as we work together to help our Afghan colleagues bring peace and security to this great nation, we must always try to understand each other as friends, partners, and, most importantly, fellow human beings. As one of the Proverbs in the book states, "Dil ba dil roh darad" (دل به دل راه دارد) - "There is a way from heart to heart."

I hope you enjoy the book as much as I have.

General David H. Petraeus
Commander, NATO International
Security Assistance Force
and U.S. Forces-Afghanistan

The original foreword in English

مقدمه

Preface to the Third Edition

A SERIES OF FORTUNATE EVENTS

Zarbul Masalha means "Proverbs" in Dari, and it was only through luck, coincidence and a chain of unusual circumstances that I ever wrote books of them at all. What began in 2010 as a personal language learning technique during a military mission in Afghanistan evolved into a hobby, then a passion, then a series of books. Five years later these books have matured into an unexpected worldwide phenomenon with readers, fans and followers in over 100 countries on six continents, and eight international book awards as of early 2015.

I deployed to Afghanistan as a U.S. Navy officer during the 2010 "surge" in American forces there. Although I joined over 100,000 U.S., NATO and International Security Assistance Force (ISAF) troops in country that year, I also was part of a very tiny minority. This was because I had learned to speak Dari (also known as Afghan Farsi) and had studied Afghan culture as part of the first wave of an experimental military program created by the U.S. Joint Chiefs of Staff.

I spent half of 2010 and almost all of 2011 in Afghanistan embedded with Afghan military, police and civilians. This included a year on President Hamid Karzai's staff inside the Afghan Presidential Palace, where I helped build and lead the first Afghan Presidential Information Coordination Center (PICC). I worked "outside the wire" every day with Afghans in their own language, and quickly became fascinated by the way most Afghans use *zarbul masalha* (pronounced "zar-bull mah-sal-HAA") in their daily speech and conversations. Afghans use proverbs and sayings far more often than Westerners do, and with far greater effect.

I learned through experience that although Afghan Proverbs were not magic spells, an appropriate one inserted at the right time in a conversation could carry the weight of an entire explanation or discussion. As a new speaker of Dari, I also found that I could "up my game" in the language by using *zarbul masalha* as shorthand for deep or important thoughts. The proverbs were easy to remember, and often even rhymed.

Afghan children learn Proverbs at a very early age

But the human factor was the most important part. Proverbial sayings and metaphors are a universal language found in every culture, and because of this I found that I usually understood the meanings of Afghan Proverbs intuitively and immediately. I saw that using them made it easier to communicate my thoughts, ideas, opinions and emotions, and that in turn led to faster, deeper human connections with my Afghan co-workers and friends. Using Afghan Proverbs helped me build my Dari vocabulary and language ability in a fun and interesting way, and led to even more conversations with Afghans. If nothing else, *zarbul masalha* were an instant ice-breaker in almost any situation.

So I started using *zarbul masalha* myself every day with Afghans in my personal and professional life. I also translated the Proverbs into English, and kept a running list of them as a language and cultural learning tool. My list grew long, and word of it spread.

Soon Afghans and foreigners alike began asking me for copies of my list. Then one afternoon, over a *chelam* (hookah) of apple tobacco with some Afghan friends at a teahouse near Bande Qargah, someone suggested I turn my list of proverbs into a book.

I had read Asne Seierstad's *The Bookseller of Kabul*, and that was all I knew about the book business in Afghanistan. But I figured it would not be too hard to find an Afghan printer in Kabul to publish a few books as a limited edition for friends and family.

Then through a chance meeting, I discovered an intrepid Kabul high school that offered to illustrate my collection.

AN AFGHAN HIGH SCHOOL PAINTS THE PROVERBS

The school was **Marefat High School (MHS)**, a progressive community-led school in the Dashti Barchi district on the southwest edge of Kabul. MHS served the local neighborhood, which was mostly of Hazara ethnicity, and was proud of teaching male and female students in the same school. That in itself was noteworthy in Afghanistan, where most schools still taught boys and girls separately. After touring Marefat, meeting the faculty, and trading some entertaining *zarbul masalha* with the students, I knew I was in the right place.

The student illustrators of Zarbul Masalha (p. 219)

Aziz Royesh, one of Marefat's founders and a civics teacher, had proposed that MHS publish my bilingual Dari-English list of *zarbul masalha*, which by now numbered well over two hundred. Aziz suggested that the MHS Art Department could hold a student contest to paint fifty proverbs from my list as part of its 2010-2011 winter semester curriculum, and that we could include these paintings in my book. MHS art teachers loved the idea of having students from 9th through 11th grades put their original interpretations of the Proverbs on canvas. I was sold.

We went even further as our collaboration progressed. On its own initiative, MHS applied for and received a small U.S. Department of State grant to publish my collection as an illustrated book, and then to distribute it at no cost to schools all over Afghanistan. I was thrilled that the results of my hobby would be used to help Afghan students learn English and Dari, and was pleased to give Marefat the rights to publish my manuscript in Afghanistan. Aziz offered to serve as editor, and we began work.

The first Dari-English edition of Zarbul Masalha (2011, Kabul)
opened left-to-right, as books published in Afghanistan do.

The book remained a personal project, not a military one. Whenever I had some off-duty time I crossed the city of Kabul to visit my new friends at Marefat High School. I had settled on 151 of my favorite and most useful proverbs, and spent many fascinating hours with Aziz and MHS art master **Hadi Rahnarwad** reviewing over 250 student proposals for illustrating 50 proverbs from my list.

The art that these talented students created appears in this book and in its companion volume, *Afghan Proverbs Illustrated.* More about Marefat High School on page 211.

GLOBAL GROWTH OF AFGHAN PROVERBS BEGINS

We finished *Zarbul Masalha* in the summer of 2011. **Karwan Press**, a small Afghan-owned and operated printer in Kabul, published 40,000 copies of the first edition. MHS distributed the books to over 200 schools across Afghanistan, fulfilling the DoS grant terms. Afghan students throughout the country began using the books to study both Dari and English.

There had been some media coverage of the project, and word continued to spread. I was particularly thrilled that the legendary **Nancy Hatch Dupree** had become a friend and supporter, and that her **Afghanistan Centre at Kabul University (ACKU)** distributed hundreds of copies of *Zarbul Masalha* to small villages throughout Afghanistan. This was accomplished through ACKU's nationwide 'books-in-a box' mobile library program called the **ACKU Boxed Library Extension**, better known as **ABLE**.

Edward Zellem, Aziz Royesh, Nancy Dupree, and ACKU staff with an ABLE mobile library box. A copy of Zarbul Masalha and Afghan Proverbs Illustrated is in each of over 200 ABLE boxes that ACKU rotates among Afghan villages.

However, my time in Afghanistan was coming to an end. After nearly a year and a half away from home, I returned to other military duties in the United States at the end of 2011.

Books were delivered to over 200 Afghan schools

Yet even back home in the United States, Afghan Proverbs stayed on my mind. I knew their importance *inside* Afghanistan, but it seemed that no one *outside* Afghanistan had heard of them except for members of the Afghan diaspora.

I was sure that non-Afghans would like the proverbs too, and would benefit from them just as I had. So I decided to share the wisdom of Afghan Proverbs with the rest of the world, and in 2012 published the second edition of *Zarbul Masalha* internationally.

People around the world were excited by the second edition, and many found unique and unexpected uses for it. In Greece, **Marina Mogli** began using *Zarbul Masalha* at an immigration center to help integrate Afghan refugees and immigrants into Greek society; like Afghanistan, Greece has a tradition of proverbs that traces back to antiquity. In Kabul, a young Afghan woman built a small public reading room and used dozens of copies to attract readers and promote Afghan youth literacy. In the United States,

Afghan Student Associations at universities in Virginia and California featured the book at fundraising events, and other Afghan community organizations and charities across the country soon followed suit. *Zarbul Masalha* was featured in more than 30 television, radio and print media stories ranging from the **BBC** and **Voice of America** to **The Christian Science Monitor**, the **Veterans Radio Network**, and **Payam-e Afghan TV**.

The second edition of Zarbul Masalha (2012)

Members of the Afghan diaspora were particularly fascinated by the book project and its impact. This was especially true of Afghan émigré parents of young children born outside Afghanistan, who wanted them to learn more about their homeland and its traditions. Many of them asked for a large-print, full-color edition to help their children learn Dari and other languages. This became *Afghan Proverbs Illustrated* in Dari and English, which soon grew into a series published in additional languages.

AFGHAN PROVERBS ILLUSTRATED

After the English-Dari edition of *Afghan Proverbs Illustrated* was published in 2012, volunteers from around the world began offering to translate it into their own native languages. This became a series of Afghan Proverbs books in a dozen third languages, including German, Dutch, French, Swedish, Greek, Spanish, Italian, Portuguese, Russian, Finnish, Polish, and Romanian (see p.220-221). As of this writing, Serbian and Korean editions are in development, and more third-language editions are planned.

Like *Zarbul Masalha*, the *Afghan Proverbs Illustrated* series is available in over 100 countries through Amazon.com, Barnes & Noble, The Book Depository, uRead, and many other leading international booksellers. Current news and details are available at www.afghansayings.com.

Afghan Proverbs Illustrated (2012)

PAREMIOLOGY

As a result of the books' growing popularity, professors and academic researchers in the field of *paremiology* began to take note. At first, I didn't even know what paremiology was. I learned that paremiology is the *scientific study of proverbs*, a sub-specialty of ethnolinguistic and folklore studies found at universities and other centers of learning all over the world. In 2013, I was honored with election to the prestigious **Associação Internacional de Paremiologia** (International Association of Paremiology/AIP-IAP). The AIP-IAP is headquartered in Tavira, Portugal, a city known internationally as 'The World Capital of Proverbs' (more on p. 214).

Because of the growing attention being paid to Afghan Proverbs, AIP-IAP president **Dr. Rui Soares** invited me to formally present my work to the AIP-IAP's **7th Annual Interdisciplinary Colloquium on Proverbs 2013 (ICP-13)** in Tavira. Delegates representing 22 nations were interested, because to date so little formal paremiological or *paremiographical* (proverb collection) work has been done with Afghan Proverbs. As a result of these books, that is beginning to change.

THE PASHTO PROVERBS PROJECT

Afghanistan has two official languages, Dari and Pashto. About half of all Afghans speak Pashto as their first language. There also are millions of Pashto speakers living just across Afghanistan's southern border with Pakistan. As the Dari Proverbs books continued gaining global attention, I often encountered a question from Pashtuns: *when will you publish a book of Pashto Proverbs?*

I had been expecting this question. I knew that *mataluna* ("Proverbs" in Pashto) are just as vital and commonly used in the Pashto language as *zarbul masalha* are in the Dari language. But there were two significant challenges. First, I was not a Pashto speaker; second, I was no longer in Afghanistan. So I developed a 21st century answer to these dual hurdles of language and geography.

The answer also became what appears to be a largely new and unexplored paremiological methodology: ***crowdsourcing for*** *content* using social media, the Internet, and mobile phones in particular. Although most Afghans in Afghanistan still lack regular access to desktop computers and high-speed Internet, millions have mobile phones – and increasingly, smartphones. This connectivity allowed me to interact online with Afghans, both in Afghanistan and around the world, through Twitter, Facebook and other social media in what I dubbed *The Pashto Proverbs Project*, which began in 2013.

Mataluna (2014) is the world's first crowdsourced collection of Pashto Proverbs

CROWDSOURCING PASHTO PROVERBS

Crowdsourcing is an online method of collecting things that became popular online in the early 21st century. It typically manifests as a way to raise money for individual or small group projects by soliciting small donations from large "crowds" of people assembled via the Internet.

However, what I needed most to write a bilingual book of Pashto Proverbs wasn't *money*, it was *content* – the Proverbs themselves. The *mataluna* had to be in common use by Afghan Pashtuns today, and there had to be exactly 151 of them to match the number of proverbs in *Zarbul Masalha*.

Thanks to the earlier books' successes and a growing global network through my book website (**www.afghansayings.com**), Twitter (**@afghansayings**), and Facebook, I already had a large and active online base. So I created an experimental *mataluna* collection page on my website, and began crowdsourcing.

Soon many fresh and popular contributions of Pashto Proverbs started flowing in. They came from native Pashto speakers in Afghanistan, Pakistan, and many other nations across six continents. Soon I had far more *mataluna* than the 151 that I needed, and I experimented with social media to test and validate them. The results were promising. For example, I learned that I could assess if a particular *matal* was popular and correctly translated by observing the number of online retweets, likes, favorites, and comments it received in social media.

THE PAREMIOLOGICAL MINIMUM

This crowdsourcing and social media methodology that I developed also helped me to judge whether a particular proverb, either in Dari or in Pashto, met the conditions of the **paremiological minimum**. This topic is of great interest to the AIP-IAP and to the paremiological community at large. This concept is attributed to the Russian paremiologist Grigorii Permyakov, who defined it in 1979 as *the core baseline of proverbs that almost all members of a society can be expected to know*. For example, most adult Americans are familiar with the proverb "the squeaky wheel gets the grease," so that proverb is considered part of the American paremiological minimum.

Features of a proverb in a culture's assessed paremiological minimum include **traditionality**, **frequency**, **familiarity** and **currency.** According to leading paremiologists, the social media methodology developed during my Pashto Proverbs project can help measure these characteristics of proverbs, and can lead to a better understanding of *any* culture's paremiological minimum. As **Dr. Peter Unseth** of the **Graduate Institute of Applied Linguistics** in Dallas, Texas has suggested, more academic work can and should be done in this area. I continue to explore the Afghan paremiological minimum in social media, and encourage others to do so.

MATALUNA: 151 AFGHAN PASHTO PROVERBS

I found an expert editor for my new *mataluna* collection in **Hares Ahmadzai**, a native Afghan Pashto speaker who also is fluent in several other languages. He generously volunteered his services to the project. By early 2014, we had selected and validated 151 of the best crowdsourced Afghan Pashto Proverbs.

Class change at Marefat High School, Kabul

I was still in touch with Marefat High School (MHS) and Aziz Royesh in Kabul. After our earlier successes with the Dari Proverbs books, Aziz and the faculty and students at MHS were as excited as I was about creating a companion book of Pashto Proverbs.

Repeating the model we used for *Zarbul Masalha*, MHS faculty and students selected 50 of their favorite *mataluna* from my list, and painting them became part of the Art Department's Fall 2013 curriculum. In addition to being another fun and interesting learning experience for the students, Marefat's "Charity Box" student aid fund was replenished with royalties from the earlier books. This helped provide tuition assistance for some of Marefat's neediest students.

The result of this unprecedented international team – the native Pashto speakers on six continents who contributed crowdsourced *mataluna*, a talented and dedicated editor, and the student illustrators and faculty of Marefat High School in our second major collaboration – became *Mataluna: 151 Afghan Pashto Proverbs*, published in July 2014.

THE BONUS PROVERBS

An unexpected benefit of the *Mataluna* crowdsourcing effort is the addition of **50 Dari "Bonus Proverbs"** in this third edition of *Zarbul Masalha*. As social media sharing grew during the Pashto Proverbs crowdsourcing effort, Dari speakers joined in and began sending me their favorite Dari Proverbs. Fifty of the most popular are featured on pages 155-204, increasing the total number of Dari Proverbs in this edition to 201.

The reader may ask why a book titled *151 Dari Proverbs* actually has *201* proverbs in it. I chose to publish this third edition with the original title to maintain continuity with the first and second editions, and to honor my original collaboration with Marefat High School. The curious reader will find more explanations in the *zarbul masalha* on pages 126 and 182.

BOOK AWARDS

The Afghan Proverbs books have won a variety of national and international awards, and I have accepted each of them on behalf of all Afghans and the student illustrators at Marefat High School. As of early 2015, awards include:

Zarbul Masalha: 151 Afghan Dari Proverbs
- Gold Medal, **Military Writers Society of America** (2013, Reference)
- Winner, **Reader's Favorite Book Awards** (2014, Nonfiction-Multicultural)

Afghan Proverbs Illustrated
- First Place, **21ˢᵗ Annual Writer's Digest Self-Published Book Awards** (2013, Reference)
- IPPY Bronze Medal, **18ᵗʰ Annual Independent Publisher Book Awards** (2014, Multicultural Nonfiction, Juvenile/Young Adult).

Mataluna: 151 Afghan Pashto Proverbs
- Finalist, **USA Best Book Awards** (2014, Nonfiction Multicultural)
- First Place, **London Book Festival** (2014, "Wild Card" category)
- Winner, **Beverly Hills Book Awards** (2015, Multicultural Nonfiction)
- Silver Medal, **IBPA Benjamin Franklin Awards** (2015, Multicultural)

ACKNOWLEDGEMENTS AND TASHAKUR (*THANKS*)

به یک گل، بهار نمی‌شه.

Ba yak gul, bahaar na-meysha.
One flower doesn't bring spring. (p. 115)

As we enter the fifth year of my work with Afghan Proverbs, there are so many "flowers" who brought spring to the project that it is impossible to list them all by name. They know who they are, and I am greatly in their debt. Their generosity of spirit and action in support of Afghan literacy, languages and communication between cultures moves and humbles me.

I particularly would like to thank the following individuals and organizations:

- The faculty, parents and student artists of **Marefat High School** in Kabul, who helped bring these books to life.
- My dear friend and editor **Aziz Royesh**, a founder and faculty member of Marefat High School and an emerging national and international voice for peace, education and development in Afghanistan (see p. 213).
- **General David H. Petraeus** (U.S. Army, Ret.), who took a personal interest in my work with Afghan Proverbs even before they were published. Now retired from military service, he wrote a brilliant Foreword to *Zarbul Masalha* in 2011 that is published for the first time in this edition. General Petraeus continues today as a great friend of Afghans and Afghan culture.
- **General John R. Allen** (USMC, Ret.), **General James N. Mattis** (USMC, Ret.), and **Nancy Dupree** of the **Afghanistan Centre at Kabul University (ACKU)**, whose early interest and encouragement remains a daily inspiration.

Aziz Royesh, Edward Zellem and General John R. Allen, USMC

- My first two Dari language instructors, **Walid Amin** and **Shakeel Anwari**, for introducing me to Dari Proverbs.
- My esteemed colleagues **Basir Ahmadi** and **Hafizullah Bayat**, who helped me refine and edit part of this collection as it first took shape.
- **Hares Ahmadzai**, the editor of *Mataluna: 151 Afghan Pashto Proverbs*, and his respected father **Major General Ghulam Sakhi Ahmadzai**, who will always be one of my dearest Afghan friends.
- Journalists **Howard Altman** (Tampa Tribune); **Cathryn J. Prince** (Christian Science Monitor); **Lina Rozbih** and **Jila Samee** (Voice of America); **Ariadne Bechthold** (Afghan Voice FM, London); **Mari Yusef** (Radio Azad); **Hadi Nili** (BBC Persian); **Amanullah Atta** (BBC Pashto); **Frank Wuco** (Fox NewsRadio); **Sahar Jaan** (Payam-e Afghan TV); **Beth Underwood** (The Blaze); **Chauncey Ross** and **Carl Kologie** (Indiana Gazette); **Dr. Farid Younos** (NOOOR-TV); **Dwight Jon Zimmerman** (Veterans Radio Network); **Malali Bashir** (Radio Free Europe/Radio Liberty) and other media personalities who have helped bring Afghan Proverbs to a global audience.
- Members of the **Associação Internacional de Paremiologia (International Association of Paremiology (AIP-IAP)** and AIP-IAP president **Dr Rui Soares**, who kindly welcomed me into their ranks and introduced me to the formal sciences of paremiology and paremiography (see p. 214).
- **Dr. Peter Unseth** of the **Graduate Institute of Applied Linguistics** in Dallas, Texas and **Dr. Wolfgang Mieder** of the **University of Vermont**. Their personal mentorship, encouragement and own scientific work in paremiology have been an education and inspiration.

- Afghan food and culture writer **Humaira Ghilzai**, who wrote a lovely Foreword to *Mataluna: 151 Afghan Pashto Proverbs*, and who inspires many around the world with her insightful essays and delicious Afghan recipes.

With the legendary Nancy Dupree in the Afghanistan Centre at Kabul University (ACKU) library, where Zarbul Masalha is in the card catalog

- The volunteer translators of *Afghan Proverbs Illustrated* from the original English-Dari into bilingual and trilingual editions in other languages. This elite international group includes **Yasamin Rahmani** (Russian); **Daniela Skirl** and **Christa Ward** (German); **Karin Johansson** (Swedish); **Marina Mogli** (Greek); **Natalie Antonowicz** (Polish); **Dr. Rui Soares** (Portuguese); **Cecilia Bernal** (Spanish); **Ariadne Bechthold** (Dutch); **Dr. Simion Cristea** and **Maria João Coutinho** (Romanian); **Dr. Liisa Granbom-Herranen** (Finnish); **Lorenzo M. Ciolfi** (Italian); **Lt Col Bertrand Voirin**, French Army (French). New editions translated by

Tatjana Šibul (Serbian) and **Jade Lee** (Korean) are in development as of this writing, and more are planned. All these books are the first of their kind in the world, and have made unique and enduring contributions to literacy and peace (see p. 220-221).

Afghan Proverbs books featured in Tavira, Portugal
"The World Capital of Proverbs"

at the 8th *Interdisciplinary Colloquium on Proverbs 2014 (ICP-14)*

Associação Internacional de Paremiologia /
International Association of Paremiology (AIP-IAP)

Dedicated to the Scientific Study of Proverbs
www.aip-iap.org

- My late mother and father, who grew to enjoy Afghan Proverbs as much as any Afghan, and my late brother **Lt. Cmdr. Scott Zellem, U.S. Navy** (1968-2004) who would have loved using Afghan Proverbs too. R.I.P.
- **Ustad Hamid Naweed**, a former art professor at Kabul University, one of the world's top Afghan art historians, an

award-winning screenwriter, author, artist, and poet, and a leading global voice for the preservation of Afghan culture and heritage.

- Afghan art master **Meena Saifi**, who painted a watercolor portrait for this book depicting renowned 19th century Afghan poet **Sufi Ashqari** (see p. 152-153).

- One of many perspectives that Afghans and Americans share is a deep and abiding love of family. Special thanks to my own family, without whose patience and support these books would never have been written.

Finally, I want to dedicate this book to all my dear and respected Afghan friends who helped me discover Afghan Proverbs, both on the ground in Afghanistan and in cyberspace. I am deeply grateful for their friendship, help and wisdom, and most of all for their efforts to build a secure and free Afghanistan. *Zenda bosheyn*! زنده باشین! Long life to you!

With best regards,
Edward Zellem
ادوارد زالم

May 2015

پیشگفتار

Introduction by
Mohammad Hussain Mohammadi

Mohammad Hussain Mohammadi is a well-known Afghan author, literary scholar and editor, and has published several acclaimed books and collections of short stories about Afghanistan. He is a winner of the Hushang Golshiris Literary Award and the Isfahan Literary Award. Many of his works have been translated into French and Italian.

Good language, the comfort of life

Proverbs make up a great part of Dari culture and folklore. Likewise, Dari folklore is a great and important part of the culture of the people of Afghanistan.

It is said that to know any people, one should become acquainted with their culture, in order to forge good relationships with them. This is because the folklore of any people shows the way they think, their rites and rituals, their mentalities, and the way they live. Moreover, in countries like Afghanistan where history often has been censored, oral history has tremendous value.

Proverbs are short, deep sentences which derive from the thoughts and wisdom of wise and unknown people. They have reached us from our ancestors, have gained popular acceptance, are used in people's everyday lives, and are regarded as part of their linguistic knowledge.

After seeing the Afghan Dari Proverbs collected and translated by Captain Zellem, I was reminded of an American woman in 1970 who for the first time had collected and published the legends of Afghanistan for children. Now, another person from the United States has collected, translated and published the Dari Proverbs. This can help the people of Afghanistan understand the viewpoints of the American people. Such research works also can help introduce the Afghan culture to Americans, and open the way for other countries to understand Afghanistan's culture.

Captain Zellem has correctly realized that "good language is the comfort of life; bad language is the enemy of life." (p. 2).

Hopefully these proverbs will be our "good language." I am grateful to Captain Zellem, who wants to extend this good language to the ears of the people of his own country.

Mohammad Hussain Mohammadi
Kabul

نکته هایی درباره ی زبان دری

Dari Language Facts

- Dari is one of the two official languages of Afghanistan; the other is Pashto. Dari is the primary language of northern, central and western Afghanistan. This includes the capital, Kabul, and the major cities of Mazar-e-Sharif and Herat.
- Unofficially, Dari is the common language used in most business and government in Afghanistan. Although statistics vary, Dari is considered to be the mother tongue of as much as 50 percent of the Afghan population.
- Dari is a very ancient and respected language, with its roots in the courts of the Sassanids (224-661 A.D.). Some call it the language of kings and priests. During this period, the Sassanids were recognized as one of the two major powers in Western Asia and Europe, along with the Roman Empire and the Byzantine Empire after Rome fell in 476 A.D.
- Dari generally is considered to be an older form of Persian Farsi, the main language of Iran. Afghans and Iranians each claim to have the more cultured dialect.
- The Dari language today remains very similar to Farsi. Although educated Dari and Farsi speakers generally have no trouble understanding each other, there are some differences in pronunciation and words. Some linguists have compared the differences between Dari and Farsi as similar to the differences between the Queen's English and Cockney or Scottish English.
- The term "Dari" was officially recognized by the Afghan government in 1964 to distinguish it from Iranian or Persian Farsi. Dari sometimes is called "Afghan Farsi" or "Dari

Persian" outside Afghanistan. It is still sometimes called "Farsi" by Dari native speakers, especially older people.

- In Afghanistan, all education above elementary school in predominantly Dari-speaking provinces is conducted in Dari, with Pashto as a language class.
- Most Afghans are bilingual to a degree in Dari and Pashto. However, it is much more common for a native Pashto speaker to speak excellent Dari than it is for a native Dari speaker to speak excellent Pashto.
- There are 32 letters in the Dari alphabet. Twenty-eight of them are shared with the Arabic alphabet. The extra four letters represent sounds that are not found in the Arabic language.
- Dari, like Arabic, is written right to left and there is no upper or lower case. Also like Arabic, Dari is written in a cursive or script style. The shapes of the letters can change depending on whether they are found at the beginning, middle or end of a word. Letters also can change shape depending on what letter combinations precede or follow them.

رهنمای تلفظ
Pronunciation Guide

Each Proverb in *Zarbul Masalha* is numbered, and is presented in at least four lines. This is useful both for language students and for general readers. The following format is used to present each entry:

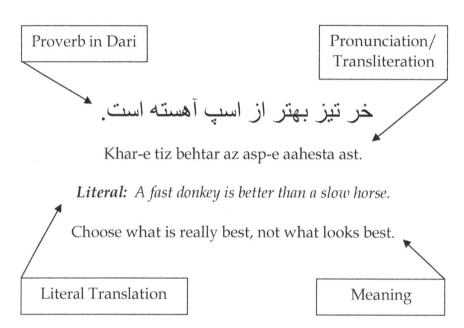

| Proverb in Dari | | Pronunciation/ Transliteration |

خر تیز بهتر از اسپ آهسته است.

Khar-e tiz behtar az asp-e aahesta ast.

Literal: *A fast donkey is better than a slow horse.*

Choose what is really best, not what looks best.

| Literal Translation | | Meaning |

رهنمای تلفظ
Phonetic Pronunciation Key

- "kh" is a "k" sound combined with an "h" sound, made in the back of the throat as if clearing it.

- "gh" is a "g" sound combined with an "h" sound, made in the back of the throat as if clearing it.

- "q" is a "q" sound combined with a soft "h" sound, made in the back of the throat as if clearing it.

- "oy" rhymes with "boy."

- "e" when attached to the end of a word sounds like "ay," as in "hay."

- "r" is a roll of the "r" sound across the tongue.

- "ey/ay"and "mey" rhymes with "hay."

- "aa" sounds like "Au," as in "August."

الفبا دری
The Dari Alphabet

ث	ت	پ	ب	ا
sey (s)	tey (t)	pey (p)	bey (b)	alef (a)

د	خ	ح	چ	ج
daal (d)	khey (kh)	hey (h)	chey (ch)	jeem (j)

س	ژ	ز	ر	ذ
seen (s)	zhey (zh)	zey (z)	rey (r)	zaal (z)

ظ	ط	ض	ص	ش
zoy (z)	toy (t)	zuwat (z)	suwat (s)	sheen (sh)

ک	ق	ف	غ	ع
kaaf (k)	qaaf (q)	fey (f)	ghayn (gh)	eyn (e)

و	ن	م	ل	گ
wow (w)	noon (n)	meem (m)	laam (l)	gaaf (g)

ی	ه
yaa (y)	hey (h or aa)

ز گهواره تا گور دانش بجوی.

Ze gahwaara taa guhr, daanesh bejoye.

Literal: *Seek knowledge from cradle to grave.*

Never stop learning, whether you are young or old.

زبان خوب راحت جان،
زبان بد دشمن جان.

Zaban-e khoob raa-hat-e jaan,
zaban-e bad doshman-e jaan.

Literal: *Good language is the comfort of life,*
bad language is the enemy of life.

A person should use clean and kind language, and not
curse or speak rudely. Speaking kindly to people
improves your life, but speaking rudely makes
enemies and will damage your life.

احترام به دیگران،
احترام به خود است.

Ehteraam ba digaraan,
ehteraam ba khod ast.

Literal: *Respect to others is respect to oneself.*

When you treat others with respect, you also
respect yourself because you are acting
with dignity and good manners.

Also: Always be respectful of other people,
if you want the same in return.

صد زدن زرگر ، یک زدن آهنگر.

Sad zadan-e zar-gar, yak zadan-e aahan-gar.

Literal: *A hundred strikes by a goldsmith,*
one strike by a blacksmith.

It is better to act with strength once and finish
something, rather than to do it weakly many times.

Also: There is a difference between the power of weak people
and strong people. For example, a hundred criticisms by an
ordinary person attract no attention — while a single criticism
made by a powerful person creates a huge impact.

خوب بپوش، خوب بخور،
زندگی کوتاه است.

Khoob be-push, khoob bukhor,
zendagee ko-tah ast.

Literal: Dress well, eat well, life is short.

Enjoy the good things in life, because
you never know when it may end.

با هر چیز بازی، با ریش بابا هم بازی.

Baa har-cheez baazi, baa reesh-e baa-baa ham baazi.

Literal: *Joking about everything, even Grandfather's beard.*

A person who takes nothing seriously and makes jokes
about everything can put himself in danger from others.
Often said to a person who is "crossing the line"
in his jokes or actions.

(English equivalent: "Playing with fire")

همه را به یک چشم نگاه کنید.

Hama-raa ba yak chashm negaah kuneed.

Literal: *Everyone should be looked at with the same eye.*

Treat everyone equally, without discrimination against
their religion, race, gender or color.

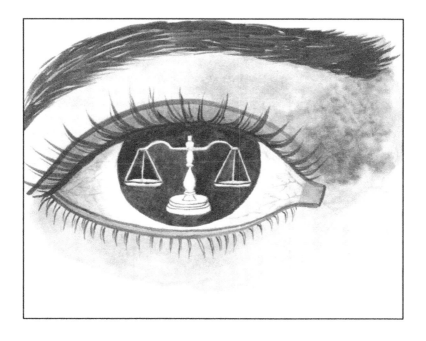

کم بخور، همیشه بخور.

Kam bukhor, hamesha bukhor.

Literal: *Eat a little, eat often.*

It is not healthy to eat too much food all at once. A person
will live longer if he eats smaller meals, but more often.

Also: It is important to be modest and careful
in spending one's resources.

مادر با یک دست گهواره ،
و با دست دیگر جهان را تکان می‌دهد.

Maadar ba yak dast gahwaara,
wa ba dast-e degar jahaan-ra takaan mey-dehad.

Literal: *Mother rocks the cradle with one hand,*
and rocks the world with the other hand.

Mothers play a very important role in the world,
and how they raise their children affects everything.

نمد سیاه به شستن سفید نمی‌شود.

Namad-e see-ya ba shustan safed na-mey-shawad.

Literal: Black carpet cannot become white by washing.

If a person is bad by nature, he cannot easily become good.
You cannot bring a bad person to the right path
by simply giving him advice.

زخم شمشیر جور می‌شه،
زخم زبان نه.

Zakhme shamsher jour mey-sha,
zakhme zabaan na.

Literal: A sword wound will heal,
  but not a wound from words.

People remember harsh statements and insults
much longer than they remember
physical pain or injuries.

یک تیر و دو نشان.

Yak teer, wa doo neshaan.

Literal: *One shot, and two targets.*

A skilled and expert person can achieve
many effects with one action.

(English equivalent: "Kill two birds with one stone.")

هر کله، بِر خیال.

Har kalaa, ber khiyal.

Literal: Different heads, different dreams.

Different people have different ideas, opinions and dreams.

*(**Note:** This proverb uses two different languages to underscore its meaning. "Har kalaa" is Dari; "ber khiyal" is Uzbeki, which is spoken in parts of northern Afghanistan.)*

(English equivalent: "Live and let live.")

گلم بیگانه تا نیم شب است.

Gelim-e begaana, ta neem-e shab ast.

Literal: Another's carpet is until midnight.

It is important to be self-reliant. A person should not count on things that do not belong to him, because eventually they have to be given back to the owner. The owner might even claim them back at an inconvenient time.

*(**Note:** Afghans often borrow carpets from their neighbors for parties and ceremonies. Of course, they must be returned when the event is finished.)*

زیبای بی‌ناز ، شوربای بی‌پیاز.

Zeybaa-ye bey naaz, shorba-ye bey peyaaz.

Literal: *Beauty without charm, soup without onion.*

If a beautiful person has no charm or manners, the beauty is useless – just as soup without onion is tasteless.

از یک دست صدا بر نمی‌خیزد.

Az yak dast sadaa bar na-mey-khizad.

Literal: From one hand comes no sound.

Just as one hand cannot clap by itself, a person cannot succeed alone. It is better to cooperate with others. Good things can happen when everyone contributes.

(English equivalent: "It takes two to tango.")

کره‌ی خر از پشت خر می‌رود ،
نه از پشت گاو.

Kora-ye khar az pushte khar mey-rawad,
na az pushte gaaw.

Literal: *The son of a donkey will follow the donkey, not a cow.*

(English equivalent: "Birds of a feather flock together.")

دهن به حلوا گفتن شیرین نمی‌شود.

Dahan ba halwa guftan sheereen na-mey-shawad.

Literal: *Your mouth cannot become sweet by saying "Halwa"*
(a traditional Afghan dessert).

You can reach your goals only by working hard,
not by talking or slogans.

(English equivalent: "Talk is cheap.")

کفش کهنه در بیابان نعمت است.

Kafsh-e kohna dar beyaabaan neamat ast.

Literal: *Old sandals are a blessing in the desert.*

Even if something is old, it is a benefit if it works and
meets your needs. Be grateful for what you have
and God will provide what you really need.

آزموده را آزمودن خطاست.

Aazmuda-ra aazmudan khatast.

Literal: *Testing of a tested one is wrong.*

It is not good to test the loyalty or disloyalty
of a person who has already proven it to you.

نیکی را نیکی، بدی را سزا.

Nekee-ra nekee, badee-ra sazaa.

Literal: Good to good, punishment to bad.

If someone is good, they will receive goodness in return.
If someone is evil, they eventually will pay a price for it.

Also: If someone treats you well, treat them well.
But if someone treats you badly, you should
find a way to avenge it.

(**Note:** *Similar to the Buddhist, Hindu
and Sikh concepts of karma.*)

کل اگر طبیب می‌بود،
سر خود دوا می‌کرد.

Kal agar tabib mey-bood,
sar-e khod dawaa mey-kard.

Literal: *If the bald man was really a doctor,*
he would have cured his own head.

This refers to a person who is pretending
to be something that he is not.

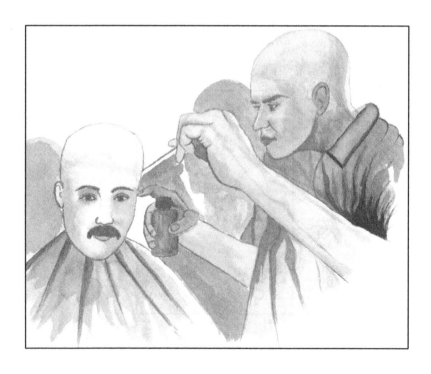

چهل درویش بر گلیمی بخسپند،
دو پادشاه در اقلیمی نگنجند.

Chehl darweysh bar gelimi bekhospand,
doo pad-shah dar eqleemee na-gonjand.

Literal: Forty darweysh can sleep on one carpet,
but two kings cannot fit in one land.

Powerful or wealthy people do not want to share their
power or wealth with anybody else. But the humble
poor (*darweysh*) have no need to compete, and so
they share what they have with each other.

از خرس موی کندن.

Az khers mui kandan.

Literal: *Pulling hair from a bear.*

It is a success to get anything from a stingy person or a cheapskate, even if it is something small. Getting something from greedy people is as hard as pulling hairs from a bear.

عیسی به دین خود، موسی به دین خود.

Isa ba deen-e khod, Mousa ba deen-e khod.

Literal: *Jesus to his religion, and Moses to his.*

All people have the right to choose what they do, think or feel.

Also: Respect and be tolerant of other religions.

جان تو جان است،
جان مه بانجان است.

Jaan-e tu jaan ast, jaan-e maa ban-jan ast.

Literal: *Your life is a life, my life is an eggplant.*

You regard your life as valuable, but don't care anything about mine. You only think about yourself and what is important to you, and do not care about me or what is important to me.

بز در غم جان کندن،
قصاب در غم چربی.

Boz dar gham-e jaan kandan,
qasaab dar gham-e charbee.

Literal: *The goat worries about his life,*
the butcher worries about the fat.

Everybody has their own problems and worries.
A person's own problems are more important
to him than someone else's problems.

بار کج به منزل نمی‌رسد.

Baar-e kaj ba manzel na-mey-rasad.

Literal: A tilted load doesn't reach its destination.

Evil always loses and good prevails. If you have bad
intentions, you ultimately will be defeated.

Also: If you try to play tricks on others,
you will pay a price in the end.

(See Appendix 1)

خربوزه از خربوزه رنگ می‌گیره.

Kharbuza az kharbuza rang mey-gera.

Literal: A melon takes its color from another melon.

A person becomes like the people he associates with.

(English equivalent: "One bad apple spoils the bunch.")

زیر کاسه، نیم کاسه است.

Zer-e kaasa, neem kaasa ast.

Literal: *Under the bowl is a little bowl.*

I think I am being tricked; there is something hidden.

اگر می‌خواهی رسوا نشوی،
همرنگ جماعت باش.

Agar mey-khwahee raswaa na-shawee,
ham-rang-e jama-at baash.

Literal: *If you don't want to become a scandal,*
be like other people.

Try to fit in, or people will gossip about you.

(English equivalent: "When in Rome, do as the Romans do.")

تا طفل گریه نکند، مادر شیر نمی‌دهد.

Ta tefl gerya nakunad, maadar sheer na-mey-dehad.

Literal: If a baby doesn't cry, the mother won't give it milk.

If you don't speak up, you won't get what you need.

(English equivalent: "A squeaky wheel gets the grease.")

قدر زر را زرگر می‌داند.

Qadr-e zar-raa zargar mey-danad.

Literal: *A goldsmith knows the value of gold.*

A wise person can see people or things
and sense their real value.

زمستان می‌رود،
سیاهی به روی ذغال می‌ماند.

Zemestaan mey-rawad,
seeya-hee ba rui zoghal mey-maanad.

Literal: Winter goes, but the charcoal's face stays black.

Don't do bad things of which you will
be ashamed in the future.

(**Note:** *Some Afghans use charcoal to heat their homes in winter.*)

نقص را از هر جایش که بگیری،
فایده است.

Noqs-raa az har jayash ke biggerie, faayidah ast.

Literal: *Stopping your losses is a gain.*

A person has to stop losing before he can win.

بز مرده شاخ زرین.

Boz-e morda shakh-e zareen.

Literal: *A dead goat has golden horns.*

When something is lost and the owner
claims much more than its real value.

تو به مه، مه به تو.

Tu ba ma, ma ba tu.

Literal: *You to me, me to you.*

If you do good things for me, I will do them for you.

Also: You protect me and I'll protect you.

(English equivalent: "You scratch my back, and I'll scratch yours.")

وقت طلا است.

Waqt telaa ast.

Literal: *Time is gold.*

Time is valuable, so use it well.

(English equivalent: "Time is money.")

مرغ او یک لنگ دارد.

Murgh-e oo yak ling darad.

Literal: *His chicken has one leg.*

Describes a person who is stubborn, and who cannot be convinced his argument is wrong.

(English equivalent: "No leg to stand on.")

چرا کاری کند عاقل که بار آرد پشیمانی.

Charaa kari kunad aaqil ke
baar aarad peshaimanee.

Literal: *Why would a wise person do*
something that brings regret.

Wise people think before they act,
so they do not have regrets later.

سر زخم نمک پاشیدن.

Saar-e zakhm namak pashidan.

Literal: To pour salt on wounds.

When someone is in pain, and someone else makes it worse.

(English equivalent is the same: "Pouring salt on a wound.")

کور خود، بینای مردم.

Kor-e khod, benaa-ye mardum.

Literal: *Blind to oneself, seeing others.*

A hypocrite cannot recognize his own faults, but has no problem pointing out the faults of other people.

از کاه ، کوه نساز.

Az kaah, koh nasaaz.

Literal: *Don't make a mountain from straw.*

Don't make something into more than it is.
Don't exaggerate.

(English equivalent:
"Don't make a mountain out of a molehill.")

سگ زرد، برادر شغال.

Saag-e zard, beraadar-e shaghaal.

Literal: *A yellow dog is the brother of a jackal.*

Bad people are all the same on the inside,
even if they look different on the outside.

از دهنش بوی شیر می‌آید.

Az dahanash bui sheer mey-aayad.

Literal: *The smell of milk comes from his mouth.*

A young, inexperienced person is not taken seriously.

سر زنده باشه، کلاه بسیار است.

Sar zenda baasha, kolaah besyaar ast.

Literal: If there is life in your head, there are lots of hats.

Being alive means you have infinite possibilities.

(See Appendix 2)

از سرناچی یک پُف است.

Az surnaachee yak puf ast.

Literal: *One blow from the trumpeter.*

This describes a person who does harm to others at little or no cost to himself, just as one blow from a trumpet can hurt someone's ears but costs the trumpeter nothing.

Also: I'll warn you or give you advice only once – you can take it or leave it.

مزاغ ، مزاغ ، کلهی زاغ.

Mazaagh, mazaagh, kala-ye zagh.

Literal: *Jokes, jokes, the crow's head.*

Making too many jokes at someone else's expense or
pushing things too far can provoke a bad reaction.

(Note: *In Dari literature, a crow often
represents a bad omen.)*

از سایه‌ی خود ترسیدن.

Az saaya-ye khod tarsidan.

Literal: Afraid of one's own shadow.

Don't be afraid or worry unnecessarily about things.

(See Appendix 3)

سزای قروت آب گرم.

Sazaa-ye qoroot aab-e garm.

Literal: The punishment for hard yogurt is hot water.

Bad people deserve harsh consequences.

*(**Note**: "Qo-root" is a ball of hard, dried yogurt that dissolves quickly in hot water. This proverb is used when a bad person gets what he deserves, which are bad consequences.*

نمک خوردن و نمکدان را شکستن.

Namak khordan wa namak-dan raa shekastan.

Literal: To eat salt and break the salt shaker.

To betray someone, forget someone's favors,
or take advantage of someone's kindness.

از کیسه‌ی خلیفه بخشیدن.

Az khesa-ye khalifa bakh-shedan.

Literal: *Offering from the Caliph's pocket.*

A person who spends from another's
pocket can be generous.

از آب گل‌آلود، ماهی می‌گیرند.

Az aab-e gel-aalud, maahee mey-gerand.

Literal: *Taking fish from muddy water.*

A person who creates confusion for his own benefit,
or profits from making trouble for other people.

گل خشک به دیوار نمی‌چسپد.

Gel-e khoshk ba dewar na-mey-chaspad.

Literal: Dry mud will not stick to a wall.

Accusations and lies without any basis
will not stick, and do not bother me.

روز ملنگ ، شو پلنگ.

Roz malang, shao palang.

Literal: *Daytime a saint, nighttime a tiger.*

A hypocrite who pretends to be a simple and pious
person, but does bad things when no one can see.

آش مردها دیر پُخته می‌شه.

Aash-e mard-haa deyr pukhta mey-sha.

Literal: *Men cook their soup late.*

Real men are not "hot-heads." They have the patience
to reach their goals, or to take revenge.

(English equivalent: "Revenge is a dish best served cold.")

پیشت بشینم، ریشت بکنم.

Peyshat bishinam, reeshat bekanam.

Literal: *I sit in front of you, and pluck out your beard.*

You are openly offending or annoying me
in my own presence.

برف بام خوده به بام ما ننداز.

Barf-e baam-e khod-a ba baam-e maa nandaaz.

Literal: *Don't throw snow from your own roof to ours.*

Don't blame us for your mistakes,
or try to pass your troubles off to us.

ضرورت مادر ایجاد است.

Zaroorat maadar-e ejaad ast.

Literal: *Need is the mother of invention.*

People are usually creative and resourceful
if they need something.

*(English equivalent is the same: "Necessity
is the mother of invention.")*

با شکم گشنه ، جنگ نمی‌شود.

Ba shikam-e gushna, jang na-mey-shawad.

Literal: *A person cannot fight when he is hungry.*

Leaders should take care of their people. People must have food in order to work, fight and survive.

هر کس را وطنش کشمیر است.

Har kas-ra watan-ash Kashmir ast.

Literal: *Everyone's homeland is Kashmir to them.*

Kashmir (a region between India and Pakistan) is considered by Afghans to be a beautiful and wonderful place. All people have an attachment to their homeland.

*(**Note:** Also commonly used in Pashto.)*

چیزی گندم تر، چیزی آسیاب کند.

Cheez-e gandom tar, cheez-e aas-yaab kund.

Literal: The wheat is a little bit wet, the millstone is a little bit dull.

Both sides are to blame for this problem.

با دُم شیر بازی کردن.

Baa dum-e sheyr baazi kardan.

Literal: *To play with the tail of a lion.*

It is not wise to provoke things that can hurt you,
or to play with dangerous things.

(English equivalent: "Don't wake a sleeping giant.")

تا جان بتن است، جان بکن است.

Ta jaan batan ast, jaan bekan ast.

Literal: *While we live, we strive.*

Life is full of challenges, and people must work hard to overcome them.

در جنگ، نان و حلوا تقسیم نمی‌شه.

Dar jang, naan wa halwaa taqsim na-meysha.

Literal: *In wartime, food and sweets are not distributed.*

People must be tough, stoic and
make sacrifices in wartime.

مشکل یک بود، ترکید دو شد.

Mushkil yak bood, tarkeed doo shud.

Literal: *One problem explodes into two.*

An unsolved problem can lead to more problems.

بنویس، بنویس، تا شوی خوش‌نویس.

Benawees, benawees, taa sha-wee khosh nawees.

Literal: *Write, write, to become a good calligrapher.*

If you work hard at something and practice,
you will become better at it.

(English equivalent: "Practice makes perfect.")

در خانه‌ی مورچه، شبنم توفان است.

Dar khaana-e murcha, shab-nam toofan ast.

Literal: *In the house of an ant,*
a dewdrop is a hurricane.

For poor people, a small loss is a big disaster.

جنگل که آتش گرفت،
تر و خشک می‌سوزد.

Jangle ke aatash gereft,
tar wa khoshk mesuzad.

*Literal: When a forest is on fire,
both wet and dry will burn.*

When there is a big problem,
both good and bad people suffer.

خر تیز بهتر از اسپ آهسته است.

Khar-e teyz behtar az asp-e aahesta ast.

Literal: *A fast donkey is better than a slow horse.*

Choose what is really best, not what looks best.

(English equivalent: "Don't judge a book by its cover.")

در نمد موی پالیدن.

Dar namad mui paaleedan.

Literal: *Looking for wool hairs in a wool carpet.*

Searching for something when there is no need
to search for it, or bringing up a problem that
everyone already knows about.

(**Note:** *Because a wool carpet is full of wool hairs,*
there is no need to look for them.)

از زیر پلو، مُلی برآمد.

Az zer-e palao, mulee bar aamad.

Literal: *From under the rice, a turnip came out.*

This is a big surprise, and not a good one.
I expected something better.

*(**Note:** "Palao" is a famous Afghan dish that includes a
delicious piece of meat buried under rice.)*

گپ از گپ تیر است.

Gap az gap teyr ast.

Literal: *The talking is beyond talking.*

It is too late, and the time is past for discussion. Everything is finished and bad things have already happened.

(English equivalent: "The train has left the station.")

تا که جوانی بکوش.

Ta ke jawaan-ee bekush.

Literal: *Strive while you are young.*

Try as hard as you can to achieve things when
you are young and have lots of energy.

جواب نادان سکوت است.

Jawaab-e nadaan sokut ast.

Literal: *The (best) answer to the ignorant is silence.*

There is no point in arguing with someone
who is being stupid and stubborn.

پشت هر تاریکی، روشنی است.

Pusht-e har taareekee, roshanee ast.

Literal: *After every darkness is light.*

Bad times will always pass,
and things will become better.

*(English equivalent: "There is a light at the
end of the tunnel.")*

در آذان ملای غریب،
کسی نماز نمی‌خواند.

Dar aazan-e mullaa-yi ghareeb,
kase namaaz na-mey-khwanad.

Literal: When the poor Mullah calls
for prayer, nobody prays.

Nobody listens to poor, helpless, or needy people.

علم تاج سر است.

Elm taaj-e sar ast.

Literal: *Knowledge is a crown on the head.*

The more you know and learn, the more
successful and respected you will be.

بهشت زیر پای مادران است.

Behesht zer-e paay-e maadaraan ast.

Literal: *Heaven is under the feet of mothers.*

Mothers have a very important role in the world,
and in the eyes of God.

آب آمد، تیمم برخاست.

Aab aamad, tayamom bar khaast.

Literal: *Water arrives, tayamom leaves.*

When there are better options, it is good
to leave lesser things behind.

Also: When a knowledgeable person arrives,
the ignorant should be turned away.

*(Note: "Tayamom" is the Islamic practice of using dust for
ritual ablutions before prayer if no water is available. When
water is available for washing oneself, dust should not be used.)*

ذغال را هر چه پکه کنی تازه می‌شود.

Zoghal-raa har che paka koni taaza mey-shawad.

Literal: *As you fan the charcoal, it becomes fresher.*

Continue to improve your skills, and
they will become even stronger.

Also: The more you learn, the more your knowledge and
wisdom will expand. Things you have learned in the past will
be refreshed, just as fanning a charcoal fire makes it hotter.

آفتاب به دو انگشت پنهان نمی‌شود.

Aaftaab ba doo angusht pen-han na-mey-shawad.

Literal: *The sun cannot be hidden by two fingers.*

Reality cannot be hidden by false explanations. The clear truth cannot be hidden, just as it is impossible to hold up two fingers and block the sun.

(English equivalent: "The truth will out.")

از ریگ روغن کشیدن.

Az reyg roghan kashee-dan.

Literal: *Extracting oil from sand.*

Describes someone who is very smart, professional,
competent or hardworking. Someone who
can create something from nothing.

(English equivalent: To take a lemon and make lemonade.")

در سختی، صبر پیشه کن.

Dar sakhtee, sabr pesha kun.

Literal: During hardship, be patient.

Be strong and have patience in difficult
times, because they will pass.

پشت آب رفته، بیل نگیر.

Pushte aab-e rafta, bel nageer.

Literal: *Don't take a shovel to bring the water back.*

When something bad happens,
don't hold a grudge – move on.

(English equivalent: "It's water under the bridge.")

صبر تلخ است، ولى برِ شيرين دارد.

Sabr talkh ast, waley bar-e shereen darad.

Literal: Waiting is bitter, but its fruit has sweetness.

It is difficult to wait for a result, but if you
have patience – good things will come.

(English equivalent: "Good things come to those who wait.")

زیبایی در سادگی است.

Zebaa-yee dar saadagee ast.

Literal: *The beauty is in the simplicity (or modesty).*

The most beautiful things often are the least complicated.

(Note: Similar to the Japanese and Zen Buddhist concepts of wabi-sabi.)

عجله کار شیطان است.

Ajala kaar-e Shaitan ast.

Literal: *Haste is the work of the Devil.*

Don't rush things if it is not necessary.
A shortcut is not always the wise solution.

(English equivalent: "Haste makes waste.")

یا تخت است، یا تابوت.

Yaa takht ast, yaa taaboot.

Literal: *Either throne, or coffin.*

I will win, or die.

(English equivalent: "It's all or nothing.")

با چل چل سگ دریا مردار نمی‌شه.

Ba chal-chal-e sag daryaa murdaar na-meysha.

Literal: A river cannot be spoiled by a dog drinking from it.

The scolding and insults of a nasty person
won't harm a good reputation.

Also: Let them say whatever they want,
it will not have any effect.

یک نه و صد آسان.

Yak na wa sad aasaan.

Literal: *One "no" and a hundred things are easy.*

It is sometimes easier to say "no" to a request and be done with it, rather than to say "yes" and take on a whole new set of problems and responsibilities.

از گپ، گپ می‌خیزد.

Az gap, gap mey-khezad.

Literal: From talk comes talk.

The more you talk about something, the more
likely it is that there will be a dispute.

*(Note: This Proverb also can be used in the opposite way, to mean
that good conversations lead to more good conversations.)*

دو ستی با مردم دانا نکوست.

Doostee baa mardum-e daanaa nekoost.

Literal: *Friendship with knowledgeable people is auspicious.*

Choose your friends wisely.

تیغ را به دست دیوانه دادن.

Tegh-raa ba dast-e daywaanah daadan.

Literal: *To give a sharp knife to the hand of a maniac.*

It is not good to give a big responsibility or power to someone who is not ready for it, or who will misuse it.

از صد خویش، یک همسایه پیش.

Az sad kheysh, yak ham-saaya peysh.

Literal: *A neighbor is closer than a hundred relatives.*

Neighbors live closest to you. If something bad happens to you, they often can help you more than your relatives can. Therefore, it is important to treat your neighbors well.

یک روز دیدی دوست،
دیگر روز دیدی برادر.

Yak roz dee-dee doost,
degar roz dee-dee baraadar.

Literal: *The first day we are friends,*
the next day we are brothers.

True friends become loyal to each other like brothers.

مشت نمونه‌ی خروار است.

Mosht namuna-ye kharwar ast.

Literal: *A handful (of wheat) is an example of the harvest.*

A small sample can show the character of the whole thing.

*(**Note:** A kharwar is a unit of measure used for crops,*
but its size can vary throughout Afghanistan.
For example: in Kabul one kharwar is 560 kilograms,
while in Ghazni one kharwar is 320 kilograms.)

(English equivalent: "A tree is known by its fruit.")

یار زنده صحبت باقی.

Yaar zenda sohbat baqee.

Literal: *As long as the friendship lives,*
there will be more conversations.

Said when parting after a good visit with a friend, or the
departure of someone you know well and respect.

از دوست یک اشاره،
از من با سر دویدن.

Az doost yak esh-ara,
az man baa sar daweedan.

Literal: *If a friend gives a signal,*
I will run with my head leading.

A person should do anything for his friend,
even at personal risk.

پایت را به اندازه‌ی گلیمت دراز کن.

Paayat-ra ba andaaza-ye gelemat daraaz kon.

Literal: *Extend your legs to the length of your carpet.*

Don't take on more than you can handle.

(English equivalent: "Don't bite off more than you can chew." Also see p. 139.)

سیرت ندیدم، سفرت پیش آمد.

Seyrat nadeedam, safarat peysh aamad.

Literal: *I am not full of seeing you,*
but the time has come for you to travel.

I wish you could stay here with me,
but I know you have to leave.

خَپ تو، چُپ من.

Khap-e tu, choap-e man.

Literal: *Your silence, my silence.*

We will both keep quiet about this – it is our secret.

(English equivalent: "Our lips are sealed")

از آنکه نمی‌دانی بدان.

Az aan-ke na-mey-danee bedaan.

Literal: *Expect the unexpected from people.*

Expect anything from other people,
even shocking or surprising things.

(English equivalent is the same: "Expect the unexpected.")

با ما نشینی ما شوی،
با دیگ نشینی سیاه شوی.

Ba ma nee-sheenee ma shawee,
ba deg nee-sheenee see-ya shawee.

Literal: *If you sit with us you will become like us, but*
if you sit with a black (dirty) pot you will become dirty.

A person becomes like the people he
associates with, either good or bad.

شراب که کهنه شود،
نشه‌ی دیگر دارد.

Sharab ke kohna shawad, nesha-ye degar daarad.

Literal: If the wine grows old, it gets you drunk differently.

Old friends and old wine are the best.

دنیا با امید زنده است.

Doonya baa omeed zenda ast.

Literal: *The world is alive with hope.*

Always have hope, because there always is hope.

دل به دل راه دارد.

Dil ba dil raah daarad.

Literal: *There is a way from heart to heart.*

Our hearts are close, we think alike,
and we are good friends to each other.

Also: We can achieve much if we work together
and trust in each other.

دشمن دانا بهتر از دوست نادان.

Doshman-e daanaa beh-tar az doost-e naadaan.

Literal: *A wise enemy is better than a foolish friend.*

A foolish friend is more dangerous to you than a
clever enemy, because you trust your friend and
he could lead you down the wrong path.

دنیا را آب بگیرد،
مرغابی را تا بند پایش است.

Doonya-ra aab biggerad,
murghabee-raa taa bande paayesh ast.

Literal: *Even if the world is covered in water,*
a duck will be on top.

Rich or powerful people have more options,
so it is easier for them to survive.

بزک، بزک، نمیر که جو لغمان می‌رسد.

Bozak, bozak, na-meer ke jaw-e Laghman mey-rasad.

Literal: *Goat, goat, don't die – the oats are arriving from Laghman.*

To give false hope to someone.

*(**Note:** Laghman province in Afghanistan is famous for its oats. This proverb refers to a legend about a farmer talking to his starving goat. He tells the goat that its food will be arriving soon, even though the farmer knows the truth that food will not come.)*

خنده نمک زندگی است.

Khanda namak-e zendagee ast.

Literal: *Laughing is the salt of life.*

Life has no flavor if you don't try to have fun.

نخوردیم از آشش،
کور شدیم از دودش.

Nakhordeym az aashesh, kor shudeym az doodesh.

Literal: We didn't eat the aash, but were blinded by the smoke.

To do all the work but receive none of the benefits,
or to pay more for something than it is worth.

(Note: Aash is a type of Afghan noodle soup, often cooked over a fire. This describes a person who stands over a fire and endures smoke to cook the aash, but doesn't get to enjoy eating it.)

شب در میان است، خدا مهربان است.

Shab dar meaan ast, Khodaa mehrabaan ast.

Literal: *Night is in between, God is merciful.*

Today may have been bad, and we don't know what will
happen tomorrow. But there is still time between today
and tomorrow. God will take care of us, so don't worry.

(See Appendix 4)

هرجا که دل برود پا می‌رود.

Har-ja ke dil berawad, paa mey-rawad.

Literal: *Wherever the heart goes, the legs go.*

Follow your intuition. Your heart
will tell you what is the right path.

به یک گل، بهار نمی‌شه.

Ba yak gul, bahaar na-meysha.

Literal: *One flower doesn't bring spring.*

You should not be content just because
one good thing happens.

Also: One person's work usually is not
enough to finish a job – it takes teamwork.

آسمان دور، زمین سخت.

Aasman duhr, zameen sakht.

Literal: *The sky is far, the earth hard.*

The situation is hopeless, a true dilemma.
There are no good options, and there is no escape.

(English equivalent: "Between the Devil and the deep blue sea.")

نان و پیاز، پیشانی باز.

Naan wa peaaz, peyshaanee baaz.

Literal: *Bread and onions and a happy forehead.*

Happy gestures are important in relations with
family or friends, no matter what there is to eat.

Also: A guest should show appreciation for any food he is
served, even if it is simple fare like bread and onions.

دیر آید، درست آید.

Deyr aayad, dorost aayad.

Literal: *Comes late, comes right.*

It is better to work slowly and well,
rather than quickly and badly.

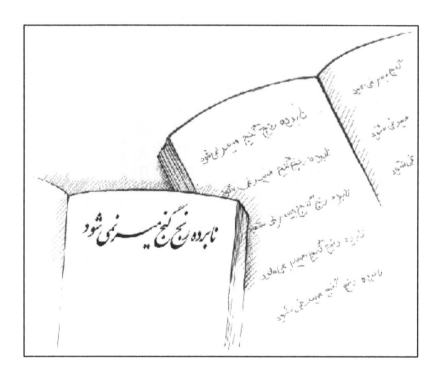

نیم نان، راحت جان.

Neem-e naan, raahat-e jaan.

Literal: *Half a loaf, but a peaceful body.*

Be content with what you have, and don't
take dangerous risks to get more.
Don't be greedy.

دیر رسیدن بهتر از نرسیدن.

Deyr raseedan behtar az na-raseedan.

Literal: *To arrive late is better than not to arrive.*

It is not good to be late, but being late
is better than not showing up at all.

(English equivalent: "Better late than never.")

آش را ناخورده، دهن سوخته.

Aash-ra naa-khorda, dahan sokhtah.

Literal: *Didn't eat the soup, but got a burned mouth.*

Describes someone who suffers or pays
a heavy price before gaining any benefit.

مهمان دوست خدا است.

Mehmaan dost-e Khodaa ast.

Literal: *Guests are friends of God.*

Always treat your guests well.

هر روز عید نیست،
که کلچه بخوری.

Har-roz eid nest, ke kulcha bukhori.

Literal: *Every day isn't Eid that you can eat cookies.*

Good opportunities don't come every
day, so make the most of them.

(**Note:** *Many cookies and treats are eaten during
the Islamic holiday of Eid.*)

(*English equivalent: "Strike while the iron is hot."*)

گل پشت و روی ندارد.

Gul pusht wa rui na-daarad.

Literal: *A flower has no front or back.*

Used to praise the overall beauty, delicacy
or symmetry of something.

Also: A polite response when a person apologizes
for having his or her back turned toward you.

الو بهتر از پلو است.

Alao behtar az palao ast.

Literal: *Warmth is better than food.*

A warm and cozy house or fireplace during winter is
one of the best things, even better than a good meal.

(**Note:** *Afghanistan is famous for harsh, cold
winters in some parts of the country.*)

برگ سبز تحفه‌ی درویش.

Barg-e sabz, tohfa-ye darweysh.

Literal: *A green leaf is the gift from a poor person.*

Said humbly when giving a small gift to someone
to show that you care for them, even though
the gift itself has little monetary value.

ماهی را هر وقت از آب بگیری، تازه است.

Maahee-raa har waqt az aab biggeree, taaza ast.

Literal: *Whenever you take a fish from the water, it is fresh.*

It is never too late to begin something new. When you begin something, it always is a fresh start.

درد هر چیز می‌رود،
درد شکم نمی‌رود.

Dard-e har-cheez mey-rawad,
dard-e shikam na-mey-rawad.

*Literal: Every pain goes away, but pain in the
stomach (hunger) never does.*

If you take someone else's food or ruin his livelihood,
that person will never forget or forgive it.

نیکی کن به دریا بینداز.

Nekee-kun ba daryaa beeandaaz.

Literal: *Do good to people, and throw your goodness in the river.*

Don't expect reward or praise for doing good things.
Do good things for their own sake, and don't
be self-satisfied or prideful about it.

(See Appendix 5)

قطره قطره دریا می‌شه.

Qattra qattra daryaa mey-sha.

Literal: *A river is made drop by drop.*

The small contributions and teamwork of ordinary
individuals can produce a big result.

Also: Don't give up – good things take time and patience.

گوسفند از پای خود کشال،
بز از پای خود.

Gosfand az paay-e khod kashaal,
boz az paay-e khod.

Literal: *The lamb will be hung by its own legs,
and the goat by its own legs.*

Everyone is responsible to themselves and to God
for what they do. God will judge everyone
according to their own actions.

*(**Note:** In Afghan markets, animals are often hung
by their hind legs for sale after butchering.)*

هم خدا خوش، هم بنده.

Ham Khodaa khosh, ham ban-dah.

Literal: *If God is happy, people are happy.*

If people do good things, it honors God
and makes Him and other people happy.

بار اسپ را بر خر گذاشتن.

Bar-e asp-ra bar khar gozaashtan.

Literal: *To put a horse's burden on a donkey's back.*

To give a professional position or
difficult task to an unqualified person.

مارگزیده از ریسمان ابلق می‌ترسد.

Maar gazida az resmaan-e ablaq mey-tarsad.

Literal: *The snakebitten are afraid of striped ropes.*

If someone has a very bad experience,
similar things can remind them of it.

(English equivalent: "Once bitten, twice shy.")

خانه‌ی گرگ بی‌استخوان نیست.

Khaanna-ye gorg bey osto-khan nest.

Literal: *A wolf's house is not without bones.*

Powerful or smart people always have backup plans
and options. They are never completely helpless,
and always have something in reserve.

کوه هر قدر بلند باشد،
سر خود راه دارد.

Koh har qadar beland baashad,
sar-e khod raah daarad.

Literal: *Even if a mountain is very high, it has a path to the top.*

Nothing is impossible; there always is a way.

صدای دهل از دور خوش است.

Sadaa-ye duhl az duhr khosh ast.

Literal: *The sound of the drum is good from afar.*

Some things or some people can seem good from a distance.
But when they are nearby, you realize they are not so good.

*(**Note:** A "duhl" is a two-sided Afghan drum*
that is very loud when it is beaten nearby.)

آب ره ندیده،
موزه ره از پا نکش.

Aab-ra na-deeda,
moza-ra az paa na-kash.

Literal: *Don't take your boots off without seeing the water.*

Don't act prematurely. Wait until the proper time.

دو تربوز به یک دست گرفته نمی‌شود.

Doo tarbuz ba yak dast gerefta na-mey-shawad.

Literal: *You can't hold two watermelons in one hand.*

Don't take on more than you can handle,
or attempt the impossible.

(English equivalent: "Don't bite off
more than you can chew." Also see p. 100.)

هر چه در دیگ است،
در کاسه می‌بر‌اید.

Har che dar deg ast,
dar kaasa mey-baraa-yad.

Literal: *Whatever is in the pot, comes on the plate.*

People usually act according to their
characters, talents and capabilities.

مزن به دروازه‌ی کسی به انگشت،
که می‌زند به دروازه‌ات به مُشت.

Mazan ba darwaaza-ye kasi ba angosht,
ke mey-zanad ba darwaaza-at ba mosht.

Literal: Don't hit someone else's door with a finger,
because your door might be hit by a fist.

Be careful not to harass or antagonize people,
because they might take revenge on you
in an even bigger way.

زور کم، قهر بسیار.

Zuhr-e kam, qahr-e besyaar.

Literal: *Little might, much fury.*

This describes a weak person who acts as if he is very powerful, or gets angry easily.

از آدم بی‌کار، خدا بیزار.

Az aadam-e be-kaar, Khodaa bey-zaar.

Literal: *God is unhappy with idle people.*

A person should work hard, be industrious, and stay busy.

(English equivalent: "Idleness is the work of the Devil.")

چاه‌کن در چاه است.

Chaah kan dar chaah ast.

Literal: Well digger is in the well.

If someone harms others, he also will be a victim.

(English equivalent: "What goes around comes around.")

از خاطر یک کیک، گلم را نسوزان.

Az khaater-e yak kaik, gelem-raa na-suzaan.

Literal: *Don't burn a carpet for a flea.*

Don't overreact to a problem, or make
a big mistake to cover a small one.

*(English equivalent: "Don't throw the baby
out with the bath water.")*

آب زور، بالا می‌رود.

Aab-e zuhr, baalaa mey-rawad.

Literal: *Water under pressure goes up.*

It is unnatural for water to flow upward. Just as it takes an external force to push water uphill, a powerful person can do things that could not be done otherwise.

گرگ در لباس چوپان.

Gorg dar lebaas-e chopaan.

Literal: *A wolf in shepherd's clothes.*

When an enemy with bad intent pretends to be harmless.

(English equivalent: "A wolf in sheep's clothing.")

طفل خورد هوشیار بهتر از کلان جاهل.

Tefl-e khord-e hoosh-yar behtar az kalaan-e jaahel.

Literal: *A smart little child is better than a foolish adult.*

A person who is clever and intelligent is more
formidable than a person who is simply strong.

(English equivalent: "Brains over brawn." Also see Proverb 181.)

پرخوری و پرگویی آبرو را می‌برد.

Poor khoree wa poor goyee aabru raa mey-barad.

Literal: Eating too much and talking too much
removes your reputation.

Being a glutton or a "chatterbox" causes
people to lose respect for you.

دیوار موش دارد، موش گوش دارد.

Deywaar moosh daarad, moosh gosh darad.

Literal: *The walls have mice, the mice have ears.*

People should keep secrets to themselves. Be careful what you say, because someone may be listening.

(English equivalent: "The walls have ears.")

بی‌شمشیر، به جنگ شیر نرو.

Bey shamshir, ba jang-e sheyr naroo.

Literal: *Without a sword, don't go fight the lion.*

Don't act without thinking, or do something
dangerous without first making yourself ready.
Be prepared before you act.

Sufi Ashqari
by Meena Saifi

در باره ی صوفی غشقری
About Sufi Ashqari

Afghan graphic artist and educator **Asadullah Saifi** was born in Kabul. Civil war forced him to leave his beloved Afghanistan, and in 1994 he took his wife and four children to Pakistan where he hoped to build a better life for them. Concerned for their future and education, Asadullah resolved to establish a school in Rawalpindi that would serve to educate his children and the children of other Afghans who had fled the Afghan civil war.

Asadullah named the school *Sufi Ashqari*, after the great Afghan poet. For as long as he lived in Rawalpindi, Asadullah kept open an educational safe haven there for Afghan refugees. Asadullah Saifi was a man who sacrificed countless hours of his life to keep the light of knowledge burning for others.

His daughter, the renowned Afghan art master **Meena Saifi**, is a great advocate of Afghan Proverbs and literacy. She has generously contributed this sketch of the Afghan poet Sufi Ashqari as a way of honoring Afghan Proverbs, and in particular to honor her father's love and commitment to education.

Asadullah Saifi presents a 5th grade certificate to his daughter Meena Saifi and her classmates at Sufi Ashqari, Rawalpindi

۵۰ ضرب المثل های اضافی

50 Bonus Dari Proverbs

Exclusive to the Third Edition (see p. xvii)

(see p. xvii)

خدا به عبادت ما محتاج نیست.

Khodaa ba ebaadat-e maa mohtaj nest.

Literal: God is not needy of our worship.

God is all-powerful, and blesses us out of His mercy alone.
He does not need us, although we need Him.

هیچ چوچه مرغی تا آخر
زیر تکری نمی مانه.

Heych choocha murghay taa aakher
zer-e tukrey na-memaana.

Literal: No chick remains under the basket forever.

Nothing remains secret or hidden forever.
Everything will be revealed at some point.

Also: Even a bad or difficult situation will pass with time.

(*Note:* Some Afghan villagers keep baby chicks under a basket
at night to protect them from cats. Although it is hard for the
chicks and they don't like it, they will not be under the basket
forever. Over time they will grow into large roosters and
chickens, and cats will no longer be a threat.)

پشه را فیل دیدن

Pasha-ra feel deedan.

Literal: *To see a mosquito as an elephant.*

To exaggerate about something, or to think that
something is bigger or more complex than it really is.

آنانی که غنی ترند، محتاج ترند.

Aa-naani-ke ghaneet-arand, muhtaaj-tarand.

Literal: *The richer they are, the needier they are.*

The more that people have, the more they want.

همه را مار خورد، ما را بقه کور.

Hama-ra maar khord, maa-ra baqa koor.

Literal: *Everyone else was bitten by a snake,*
but I was bitten by a blind frog.

This proverb describes unexpected bad luck, or a problem
with something or someone you thought was harmless.

دل تنگ نباشد، جای تنگ نیست.

Dil-e tang nabaashad, jaay-e tang nest.

Literal: If the heart isn't narrow, the place isn't narrow.

It is good to be generous, to share, and to help others.

(**Note:** *Often used when a person is looking for somewhere to sit in a bus or other crowded place, and someone kindly makes room.*)

نام رستم بهتر از رستم است.

Nam-ae Rostam behtar az Rostam ast.

Literal: *Rostam's name is better than Rostam.*

This proverb is used when a person's name or reputation is better than his actual abilities.

(**Note:** *Rostam was a legendary athlete and warrior-hero in ancient Persia. See Appendix 4.*)

از بی کفنی زنده ماندیم.

Az bey-kafani, zenda maandem.

Literal: *From the lack of a coffin, I stayed alive.*

Describes a person who is completely helpless to act,
because he has no resources or opportunity to do anything.

بترس از کسی که او نمی ترسد از خدا.

Bee-tars az kasey ke oo na-meytarsad az Khodaa.

Literal: *Fear the person who does not fear God.*

Beware of people who do not believe in God or are not afraid
of Him, because they have no limits on their actions.

خائن خائف است.

Khaayen khaayef ast.

Literal: A traitor is afraid.

A guilty person has fear inside, even if he does not show it on the outside. He pays a heavy price from his own conscience.

قصاب که زیاد شد گاو مردار میشه.

Qasaab ke zeyaad shud, gaw murdaar meysha.

Literal: *Too many butchers spoil the cow.*

If too many people are in charge of a job, sometimes nothing happens or the job is done poorly.

(English equivalent: "Too many cooks spoil the soup.")

آب از سرچشمه گِل آلود است.

Aab az sarchashma gel-aalud ast.

Literal: *The water is muddy from its source.*

Describes a bad situation that was bad from the
very beginning, or a case where people
do not trust their leaders.

ماهی از سر گنده گردد، نی از دم.

Maahee az sar ganda gardad, nay az dom.

Literal: A fish rots from the head, not from the tail.

Problems usually begin at the top.

(English equivalent is the same: "A fish rots from the head first.")

آمدم ثواب کنم، کباب شدم.

Aamadom shawaab kunum, kabab shudum.

Literal: *I came to do good things, but I became a kebab.*

When a person tries to do something good,
but ends up creating bigger problems for himself.

(*Note:* *The comparison to a kebab (grilled meat) is similar
to the English expression "getting burned.")*

(*English equivalent: "No good deed goes unpunished."*)

آنقدر ایستاده شو،
تا علف زیر پایت سبز شوه.

Aan qadar estaada-sho,
taa alaf zer-e paayet sabz shawa.

Literal: *Stand until grass grows under your feet.*

You are waiting in vain. You can stay as long as you
like, but the thing you want will never happen.

Also: I refuse to do what you want.

خود گل باشی، و عمرت نی.

Khod gul bashi, wa omret nay.

Literal: Be like a flower, but may your life be longer.

A kind thing to say when giving praise, thanks
or in farewell. Also used when giving flowers.

تا باد نباشه، بته شور نمی خوره.

Taa bad na-baasha, botta shur na-meykhora.

Literal: If there is no wind, a bush doesn't move.

There is a reason for everything. Every effect has a cause.
Things do not just happen by themselves for no reason.

صدای گوز گم می شه،
بوی گوز نه.

Sadda-ye goz-gom meysha, boyee goz na.

Literal: *You can hide the sound of a fart,*
but you can't hide its smell.

Bad deeds cannot be hidden completely. The truth
will be revealed sooner or later.

خارپشتک میگه، "بخمل بچیم."

Kharpushtak mega, "Bakhmal bachaim."

Literal: *A porcupine says, "My son is velvet."*

Used when someone cannot see the reality of his
own nature, or deceives himself about his own flaws.

Also: Parents usually see the good sides
of their own children first.

دور نرو که گرگ می خوریت،
نزدیک نیا که دیده ندارم.

Duhr naroo ke gorg meykhorit,
nazdeek-e nayaa ke deeda nadarum.

Literal: Don't go so far away that the wolf will eat you,
but don't come close enough for me to see you.

I do not particularly like you, but I do not wish bad things for
you either. This *zarbul masal* is helpful when a person has
mixed, indifferent or ambivalent feelings about someone else.

شیرِخانه، روباه بیرون.

Sher khanna, rubah beyroon.

Literal: A lion at home, and a fox outside.

A person who appears strong and powerful when
things are easy and safe, but is weak and
cowardly when it really matters.

پنج انگشت برادر است، برابر نیست.

Panj angusht braadar ast, baraabar nest.

Literal: *Five fingers are brothers, but are not equals.*

We are all human, but that does not mean we all have equal talents, gifts or rewards. Even though people may be related by family or nationality, each person is unique.

دست شکسته کار می کنه،
ولی دل شکسته نی.

Dest-e shekastah kaar meykona,
waley dil-e shekastah nay.

Literal: *A broken hand can work, but a broken heart cannot.*

A person can overcome a physical
handicap, but not a broken spirit.

برادر با برادر، حسابش برابر.

Braadar baa braadar, hesaabesh baraabar.

Literal: *Between brother and brother,*
accounts should be equal.

It is important to be honest and fair in dealing with other
people. Business always should be done fairly,
especially business between family and friends.

بخشش به خروار، حساب به مثقال.

Bakhsheesh ba kharwar, hesaab ba mashqal.

Literal: *Give by pounds, account by ounces.*

Be generous and give liberally, but do business exactly.

(**Note:** *A kharwar is an Afghan unit of measure used for crops; see the definition on p.97.*)

هیچ کس نمی گوید که،
"دوغ من ترش است."

Heych-kas na-meygoyad ke, "Dogh-e man torsh ast."

Literal: *No one says, "My own buttermilk is sour."*

People don't usually advertise their
own faults or criticize themselves.

بزرگی به عقل است، نه به سال.

Bozorg-ee ba aql ast, na ba saal.

Literal: *A person's greatness is in wisdom, not age.*

Age alone does not make wisdom. You should consider
what everyone has to say, because sometimes a smart
young person has more to offer than an older person.

(Also see Proverb #148.)

سرکه مفت از عسل شیرین تر است.

Sirkah-e muft az aasal shireen-tar ast.

Literal: *Free vinegar is sweeter than honey.*

Everyone loves getting something for nothing.

خون به خون شسته نمی شه.

Khoon ba khoon shustah na-meysha.

Literal: *Blood cannot be washed out with blood.*

One bad deed cannot be fixed by another.

(English equivalent: "Two wrongs don't make a right.")

دزد نباش، از پادشاه نترس.

Dozd na-baash, az paad-shah na-tars.

Literal: Don't be a thief, and you won't fear the king.

If you are honest, open and righteous,
you don't have to be afraid of anything.

خدا را نمی بینیم، اما با دلیل می شناسیم.

Khodaa-ra na-meybeeneym, amah ba dalil mey-shnaseym.

*Literal: We don't see God, but we can
know him through His signs.*

This proverb is used to persuade someone of a truth that
cannot be easily seen or believed. Just because you cannot
see something does not mean that it is not there.

Also: Can be used when commenting on
someone's honesty, treachery, or overall character.

دروغ گو حافظه ندارد.

Drogh-goy-e haafez-a nadarad.

Literal: *A liar has no memory.*

Eventually a dishonest person cannot remember all his own lies, and therefore cannot be consistent in his lying.

گذشته را صلوات، آینده را احتیاط.

Gozashtah-ra salawat, aayendah-ra aahatyas.

Literal: Forget the past, be vigilant about the future.

What has happened cannot be changed. However, you should use lessons from history and your experience to succeed.

*(**Note:** "Salawat" is to pray a special Islamic prayer. When Afghans want to ease tensions or make peace, they sometimes ask people to do a salawat and forget their disputes. This can help everyone to move past old problems and be more careful about the future.)*

(English equivalent: "Let bygones be bygones.")

دویدن، افتادن هم دارد.

Daweedan, aaftaa-dan ham darad.

Literal: *To run is also to fall.*

Be careful, because prosperity also can bring danger. If you dare greatly, you also should be prepared to fail greatly. Sometimes there is a price to pay for success.

جوینده یابنده است.

Joyenda yaabeenda ast.

Literal: *The seeker is the finder.*

The harder you look for something,
the more likely you are to find it.

(English equivalent: "Seek and ye shall find.")

نام بلند بهتر از از بام بلند است.

Nam-e beland behtar az bam-e beland ast.

Literal: *A high name is better than a high roof.*

Having a good reputation is true wealth. It is much better than having an expensive house or other material riches.

مشت پُر باشد، پُر زنبور باشد.

Mosht pur baashad, pur zanboor baashad.

Literal: *A hand should be full, even if it is full of wasps.*

Having something is better than having nothing.
Even a handful of stinging wasps is better
than a handful of nothing.

تا احمق در جهان است،
مفلس در نمی ماند.

Taa ah-maq dar jahan ast,
muflis dar na-meymaanad.

Literal: *As long as there are fools in the world,
a pauper will not stay helpless.*

A fool will spend his money on anything. It is easy
for people to take advantage of a foolish person.

(English equivalent: "A fool and his money are soon parted.")

راستی را از طفل بپرس.

Rastee-ra az tefl bee-purs.

Literal: Ask the truth from a child.

An innocent child will give a true answer.

(English equivalent: "Out of the mouths of babes.")

خدا که میدهد، نمی پرسد
که بچۀ کی هستی.

Khodaa ke mey-dehad, namey-purseed
ke bacha kee hastee.

Literal: When God gives, He doesn't ask
whose son a person is.

God blesses people without regard for rank or importance.

آنچه دلم خواست نه آن شد؛
آنچه خدا خواست همان شد.

Aan-che dil-am khwast na aan shud;
aan-cha Khodaa khwast haman shud.

Literal: *What my heart wanted didn't happen;*
what God wanted was actually done.

God knows what is best for us, even if we do not. He
sometimes works in ways that we don't understand.

(English equivalent: "Man proposes, God disposes.")

کابل بی زر باشد، بی برف نی.

Kabul bey-zar baashad, bey-barf nay.

Literal: *May Kabul be without gold,*
rather than without snow.

Snow on the mountains around Kabul is more valuable
to Afghans than gold, because when the snow melts
it creates the water that people need to live.

دوای دندو، کندو یه.

Dawa-ye dandoo, kandoo ya.

Literal: The cure for a bad tooth is extraction.

Sometimes the only solution to a problem is to eliminate the problem instead of fixing it.

(**Note:** *This proverb is mostly used in Hazaragi local dialects, which are closely related to standard Dari.)*

عذر بدتر از گناه.

Ozri bad-tar az goonaah.

Literal: The excuse is worse than the sin.

This proverb is used when people offer lies or weak
apologies to explain their mistakes, and as a
result make things even worse.

(English equivalent: "If you're explaining, you're losing.")

هیچ کس نخارد پشت من،
جز ناخن انگشت من.

Heych-kas na-kharad pushti man,
joz na-khani angoshti man.

Literal: *Nothing will scratch my back except my own finger.*

It is important to be self-reliant. The only people you
can truly count on in hard times are yourself and
the people who are closest to you.

آسیابان سگی داشت؛
سگ او سگی داشت.

Asya-baan saag-e dasht; saag-e oo saag-e dasht.

Literal: The miller had a dog; his dog had a dog.

This proverb is used with contempt when someone blindly follows the orders of another person's servant or puppet.

گره که به دست باز شود،
حاجت به دندان نیست.

Gereh ke ba dast baaz shawad,
hajat ba dan-dan nest.

*Literal: If a knot can be opened by the hand,
there is no need for the tooth.*

Look for the simplest and most effective way to solve
problems. If there is an easy way to repair something, do it
that way. There is no need to take on a heavier burden or
make things more complicated than they need to be.

تخته که به تخته جور آمد،
حاجت نجار نیست.

Takhta ke ba takhta jor aamad, hajat-e najar nest.

Literal: It two pieces of wood fit together,
there is no need for a carpenter.

Try to do things yourself if you can. If you can
fix a problem yourself, there is no need
to seek help from others.

هر کی بامش بیش، برفش بیش.

Har-ke bamash bish, barfash bish.

Literal: *A person with a wide roof has more snow on it.*

Wealthy or powerful people have more things, but they also have more expenses and more responsibility to society.

(English equivalent: "To whom much is given, much is expected.")

کوه به کوه نمی رسد،
آدم به آدم می رسد.

Koh ba koh na-meyrasad,
aadam ba aadam meyrasad.

Literal: Mountains do not come closer together, but people do.

Don't be upset or sad if you are far from your friend,
family or lover, because you will meet again someday.

Also: People with compatible natures can connect
emotionally even if they are far away from each other.

This Proverb refers to a Dari fable about a goose and a fox who liked to play tricks. One day the fox invited the goose for lunch. When the goose came, the fox served him soup on a plate. The goose could not eat it because the plate was flat and he had a long beak. So the fox ate all the soup himself, and then smugly asked the goose if the soup was delicious. The goose was annoyed. He thanked the fox and invited him to come for lunch the next day.

The fox didn't eat anything the next morning. At noon he rushed to the goose's house. The goose served the fox a meal in a jar with a long neck. The fox could not eat anything, because his short nose would not fit in the jar. So the goose used its long beak to eat all the food in the jar. Then with a knowing smile, the goose smugly asked the fox if the food was delicious.

The fox understood the revenge of the goose, thanked him, and ran home to find something to eat.

Appendix 2
(Proverb #46)

This Proverb refers to a Dari fable about a man with a favorite hat that he had loved all his life. One day, passing a mountainous path, he encountered a thief who wanted to rob him of everything – including his treasured hat. The man thought for a moment, handed his hat to the thief, and said, "If you let me keep my head, I can always get another hat."

Hearing this, the thief asked him about the secret of his words. The man said that he loved his hat, but he loved his life more than the hat. The thief had mercy because of his wise words, and returned the man's hat and all his other belongings.

Rostam was a legendary athlete and warrior-hero in ancient Persia. He heard news of another famous athlete named Sohrab, who lived in a rival kingdom. Rostam was jealous, angry and afraid. He searched for Sohrab because he could not tolerate any competitor equal to himself.

Eventually Rostam and Sohrab met on a battlefield, but neither knew the other's identity. Based on old stories from his mother Tahmina, Sohrab began to suspect that his opponent might be Rostam, his long-lost father. Because of this, Sohrab fought Rostam reluctantly and without vigor.

The two men fought for three days. Eventually, Rostam gained the upper hand and killed Sohrab with a knife. As Sohrab was dying, he threatened Rostam with the revenge of his father. Rostam demanded to know who Sohrab's father was. Sohrab said, "My father is Rostam."

Rostam was shocked, and demanded proof. Sohrab showed him a token that his true father once had given Tahmina. Rostam recognized the token, and was heartbroken. He now knew that he had killed his own son, and without reason had feared him as a rival.

This Proverb refers to a Dari fable about an innocent man who was imprisoned unfairly. One evening the news came to him that he had been sentenced to death and would be executed in the morning.

The man was very afraid. But he trusted in God and said, "I may hang tomorrow, but there is still one night in between, and God is merciful."

The next day, he was taken to the public square to be hung. Suddenly, the King passed by and asked about the noise of the crowd. When he was told the name of the man about to be executed, the King exclaimed, "Oh, no! Haven't they received my last order? I found him innocent and sent a message not to punish him."

And the man was set free, and thanked God.

This Proverb refers to a Dari fable from the time of an Abassid Caliph. A kind and pious man had the habit of visiting the river every day. Each day the man would honor God by throwing a small package of food into the river, in the hope that it would be found by some needy person or animal.

One day, the Caliph's beloved son went to the river alone to swim. He was swept away by its strong currents. Fate brought him ashore on a deserted beach. There was nothing to eat and he expected to die.

However, every day a package of food from the faithful man washed onto the beach and gave the young prince sustenance. After a few days, the Caliph's men found the prince and brought him back to the Palace.

The Caliph thanked God, and sent his men to find the person who had been throwing food into the river. When they found the pious man, they brought him to the Palace. The Caliph rewarded him with gold and many other gifts.

درباره ی مولف
About the Author

Captain Edward Zellem has served as a United States Navy officer for 28 years. He began studying Dari in early 2010, and soon became captivated by the profound meanings and colorfulness of Afghan Proverbs. He started collecting them as a hobby and to help with his language studies.

After deploying to Afghanistan later that year, he worked for a year and a half embedded with Afghans in Kabul and Kandahar, including a year on President Hamid Karzai's staff inside the Presidential Palace of Afghanistan. Meanwhile, he continued to collect Afghan Proverbs as he heard and used them in his daily life.

After students at Marefat High School in Kabul offered to create illustrations, he decided to publish his collection and share it with the world. This became the award-winning books *Zarbul Masalha: 151 Afghan Dari Proverbs*, the *Afghan Proverbs Illustrated* children's series in over a dozen languages, and *Mataluna: 151 Afghan Pashto Proverbs*.

He has won a variety of international awards (see p. xvii) for his bilingual books of Afghan Proverbs. The books are a personal project to support Afghan literacy and cross-cultural understanding, and to demonstrate our common humanity.

Captain Zellem at Marefat High School, Kabul

در باره ی معرفت

About Marefat High School

Marefat High School (MHS) was founded in 1994 in Pakistan to educate Afghan refugees. By 2001, more than 6000 Afghan male and female students were enrolled in different branches of the school in the cities of Rawalpindi, Attock, and Peshawar. At the beginning of the new political era in Afghanistan in 2001, MHS moved to Kabul and began educational programs in the 13th District, also known as Dashti Barchi – one of the poorest areas of the city.

Marefat High School, Kabul

Today, (2015) MHS has more than 3000 students enrolled. Since 2006, 100% of its graduates have successfully entered Afghan universities and other higher education institutions. More than 120 students have received scholarships for higher education in different countries around the world. For three successive years

Marefat High School has been ranked #1 in Afghanistan's nationwide university entrance exams; this achievement has made Afghan history in the modern era. MHS is one of the brightest beacons of hope in the entire Afghan educational system, even surpassing schools in wealthier areas that are far better funded and equipped.

Directed by a Board of Trustees, MHS is regarded as a model non-profit community initiative that provides quality education for Afghan children. Infrastructure, equipment, and the budget of the school are funded by a small tuition fee from each student. This is supplemented by contributions from Board members and other charitable donors from the community.

As of 2015, tuition at Marefat High School is approximately $230 U.S. dollars for an entire year, including books. Many Afghan families struggle to pay even this amount. Annually, private donors sponsor the educational expenses of more than 400 students in need through the "Marefat Charity Box."

MHS has nurtured many bright young talents in the fine arts, including painting, music, theater, story-writing, and poetry. One of the most successful projects by MHS students has been their illustration of Captain Zellem's *Zarbul Masalha* and *Mataluna* collections, with 50 works of original art in each book. The illustrations were created by young student artists between the ages of 14 and 16 in grades 7 to 10, guided by Marefat art masters and other faculty.

Progressive, integrated, community-based schools such as Marefat High School are the key to a brighter future for Afghanistan. Private and international donations to the school are always deeply appreciated.

More information about Marefat High School, including student essays and artwork, is available on its website in both Dari and English at http://www.marefatschool.org. The school's e-mail address is marefat12@gmail.com.

در باره ی ویراستار
About The Editor

Aziz Royesh is a high school teacher at Marefat High School (MHS), and is a leading advocate for equal access to primary and secondary education in Afghanistan. As a refugee himself, he founded a small school for Afghan refugees in Pakistan in 1994. The school flourished. Aziz moved the school to Kabul in 2002 after the fall of the Taliban, and it grew into today's MHS.

In addition to editing *Zarbul Masalha*, Aziz has written textbooks on humanism, human rights, democracy, social studies, and Quranic interpretation, and is a frequent speaker on the concept of a tolerant community. He has received a variety of honors for his work in education, including selection as a Yale World Fellow (2010); as a Reagan-Fascell Democracy Fellow (2011-12); and as a Top Ten World Finalist for the Varkey Foundation's prestigious Global Teacher Prize (2015). Aziz teaches civic education at MHS and is a member of Marefat's Board of Trustees.

His autobiography, *Let Me Breathe*, covers three decades of radical change in Afghanistan after the Communist coup in 1979. The Dari edition has become popular around the world, and an English translation is in progress.

در باره ی AIP-IAP
About the Associação Internacional de Paremiologia/ International Association of Paremiology (AIP-IAP)

The AIP-IAP is a non-profit cultural institution based in the city of Tavira, located in the Algarve region of southern Portugal. The Association is dedicated to *Paremiology*, the scientific study of proverbs (see p. xii). As the only association of its kind in the world, the missions and purposes of the AIP-IAP include:

- To encourage international cooperation in Paremiology and related scientific areas;
- To establish action programs with educational officials, public and private;
- To encourage young researchers who are helping to defend, preserve and promote intangible cultural heritage;
- To organize national and international conferences in Paremiology;
- To promote studies in Paremiology, the scientific study of proverbs.

The quality and quantity of AIP-IAP activities, and the published works of its members, are recognized by world-renowned experts in global proverbs such as paremiologists, phraseologists, and folklorists. This dynamism has resulted in support from the Municipality of Tavira, the Foundation for Science and Technology, the National Cultural Centre in Lisbon, the Secretary of State for Culture-Regional Directorate of Culture of the Algarve, and UNESCO, which has honored the AIP-IAP by granting it an Honorary Patronage. More information at http://www.aip-iap.org.

Recess at Marefat High School

The Art classroom

The original manuscript of *Zarbul Masalha*

Selecting illustrations

MHS presents a portrait to General David Petraeus
as thanks for his interest in *Zarbul Masalha*

With Afghan media after portrait presentation

With Afghan co-workers on a visit to Kapisa province

Afghan National Army 205th Corps soldiers in Kandahar
often use Proverbs to motivate and educate

The Artists of *Zarbul Masalha*
Marefat High School (MHS)Art Department

(*Right to Left -1st Row*): Sher Ali Hussaini, Najibullah, Salim, Ali Yasir, Qodratullah, Reza, Ehsan, and Hadi Rahnaward.
(*Right to Left - 2nd Row*): Hamid Fidel, Zainab Haidari, Tahira Jafari, Tahira Mohammadi, Fatima Rezayi, Amena Noori, and Najiba.

Aziz Royesh and Captain Zellem with MHS art students

Translations of *Afghan Proverbs Illustrated*

Now in over 100 countries

Greek

German

French

Russian

Polish

Portuguese

More Translations of *Afghan Proverbs Illustrated*

Available through Amazon and other leading booksellers

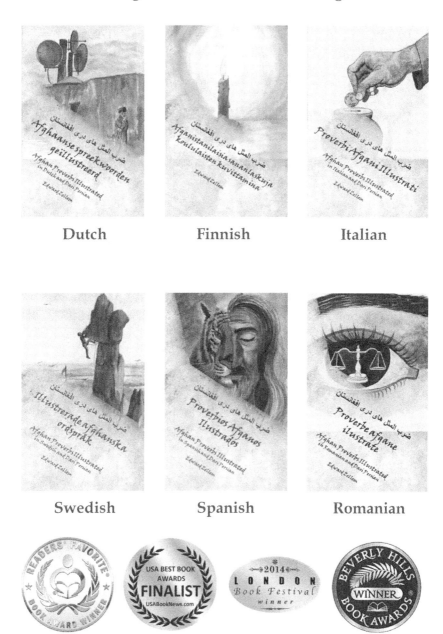

Dutch   Finnish   Italian

Swedish   Spanish   Romanian

فهرست
Index

Beauty	Zebaa-ye	زیبایی	15, 87, 124, 170
Character	Shakh-seeyat	شخصیت	10, 17, 29, 31, 34, 44, 54, 90, 97, 104, 137, 140, 142, 149, 161, 163, 164, 175, 181, 184, 185, 186, 203
Clever	Hoosh-yar	هوشیار	12, 103, 108, 148, 190, 192, 193, 201, 202
Cooperation	Ham-kaaree	همکاری	16, 23, 37, 115, 204
Creative	Aa-fareen-enda	آفریننده	59, 103, 201, 202
Danger	Khatar	خطر	47, 48, 63, 69, 92, 94, 103, 134, 138, 141, 147, 151, 188
Determination	Ba-ezm	با عزم	64, 67, 74, 81, 89, 114, 136, 201, 202
Education	Tahseel	تحصیل	1, 74, 78, 81
Effort	Talash	تلاش	18, 24, 67, 114, 127, 143, 199, 201, 202
Equality	Baraa-baree	برابری	7, 13, 176, 178, 179, 194
Exaggeration	Egh-raaq	اغراق	43, 49, 68, 71, 134, 137, 142, 145, 157, 161,175, 198
Family	Fameel	فامیل	9, 79, 173, 204
Friendship	Doostee	دوستی	92, 93, 95, 96, 98, 99, 101, 105, 107, 170, 204
Gratitude	Qadr-danee	قدر دانی	19, 111, 117, 119, 155, 182, 195
Guests	Mehmaan	مهمان	117, 120, 122, 126, 160, 170
Health	Sehat	صحت	8, 60, 125
Home	Khanna	خانه	61, 95, 125
Hope	Omeed	امید	76, 106, 110, 136, 156, 177, 204
Hypocrisy	Reyaa	ریا	27, 42, 52, 55, 158, 164, 173, 180, 198
Justice	Adalat	عدالت	21, 50, 132, 171, 178, 179, 183, 198, 203
Limits	Hud	حد	6, 73, 91, 100, 139, 163, 174, 183, 197

فهرست

Index

Loyalty	*Wafaa-daary*	وفاداری	20, 51, 99, 102, 200
Mistakes	*Ghalatee*	غلطی	99, 112, 144, 183,
Opportunity	*Forsat*	فرصت	5, 81, 123, 127, 136, 156, 162, 191, 192
Optimism	*Khosh-been*	خوشبین	76, 106, 107, 111, 136, 156, 177, 189, 195
Pain	*Dard*	درد	11, 41, 69, 84, 128, 188, 197
Patience	*Hawsela*	حوصله	56, 65, 67, 84, 86, 88, 118, 130, 138, 156, 169, 201, 204
Possibilities	*Emkaanaat*	امکانات	32, 46, 116, 127, 135, 171, 187, 192
Quality	*Kayfeeyat*	کیفیت	33, 45, 70, 80, 90, 108, 133, 137, 148, 165, 167, 175, 181
Regret	*Nedaamat*	ندامت	40, 85, 168, 187,
Respect	*Ehteraam*	احترام	2, 3, 57, 77, 78, 79, 181, 194, 200
Responsibility	*Massoul-iat*	مسئولیت	14, 62, 91, 129, 131, 144, 150, 171, 183, 199, 203
Silly	*Abla*	ابله	75, 108, 111, 192
Strong	*Qa-wee*	قوی	4, 83, 109, 135, 146, 148, 175
Successful	*Mowafaq*	موفق	35, 83, 109, 143, 188, 189, 203
Surprise	*Tajob*	تعجب	72, 103, 172
Tolerance	*Tah-mal*	تحمل	25, 174, 176, 181, 194, 195
Trickery	*Tazweer*	تزویر	22, 28, 30, 39, 53, 82, 103, 147, 172, 184, 186
Truth	*Haq-ee-qat*	حقیقت	82, 172, 179, 184, 185, 189, 193
Unfair	*Bey-ensaafanaa*	بی انصافانه	26, 58, 109, 110, 112, 121, 168, 178
Unlucky	*Chans-e-bad*	چانس بد	66, 68, 77, 116, 121, 159, 162
Value	*Arzesh*	ارزش	36, 38, 112, 166, 167, 176, 179, 182, 196

More Praise for Afghan Proverbs

"Captain Edward Zellem has written one of the most remarkable books in recent memory about Afghanistan."
Veterans Radio Network

"I love the way each proverb is laid out, first written in Dari, then the pronunciation, followed by the translation and explanation. This helps connect the proverb to the language, while making the meaning accessible to those of us who have never ventured to that part of the world."
Writer's Digest

"I can't say enough wonderful things about this book! It truly is a treasure. Edward Zellem has done an amazing job in bringing Afghanistan's heritage and culture to a global audience."
Fahim Fazli
Hollywood actor, award-winning author and combat interpreter

"This is incredible stuff. It is a huge service to the languages and proverbs in this part of the world. The narrative of peace, universal love and mutual understanding central to the idea is so beautiful."
Ali Jan
Medical doctor, historian, and grandson of Qazi Ahmad Jan

"This book helps both Afghan and non-Afghan readers to learn more about the intricacies of Afghan culture, and shows the keen observations of Edward Zellem in appreciating its true nature."
Hamid Naweed
Former Professor of Art History at Kabul University
and author of Art through the Ages in Afghanistan

"A wonderful book that every Afghan under the age of 45 should have....your mothers will be dazzled to hear you speak using Proverbs."
Humaira Ghilzai
Afghan food and culture writer
"Afghan Culture Unveiled" - www.afghancooking.net

Made in the USA
Monee, IL
26 October 2023